Dedication

To all furry family and friends who teach us how to
celebrate life with love and laughter.
A special thanks to Nick, Lexy, Whitney, Misha, and Brandy
who taught me how to
give parties to celebrate my pets.

Acknowledgements

Thanks to Carole Pivarnik for her brilliant illustrations in the book and for her advice and assistance on book layout decisions – but most of all, for her sense of humor that helped keep the project going to the finish line. Posh and I are so very grateful to Mary Beth Kvaka, the owner of Scalawags, a fabulous pet store in Kennebunkport, Maine – our official advisor on all things related to furry friends and their humans. A special thanks goes to Ron Graf, who not only suggested to Posh that he write a party guide book, but who also cheerfully read through multiple book drafts with his red editing pen! We also want to thank all of our friends and family who listened to our ideas about the book and contributed their own ideas.

Finally, I'd like to acknowledge all of the treasured pets who have graced my life since I was a little girl – Lindy, Sandy, Brandy, Misha, Whitney, Nick, Lexy, Alessandra, Zhivago – and of course, Posh. There has been no greater gift in my life than their love and friendship.

About the Authors

Posh Rogers is a 10-year old Westie with a friendly, happy attitude about life. He loves sharing good times with his family and friends, so you will always find him with a smile and a wagging tail ready to hop in his Miata and find a party. At 27 pounds, he is a "big Westie" – sturdy and handsome with the independent spirit of his breed but a heart full of love.

Susan Rogers is a tax lawyer who loves pets and parties. Posh and Susan split their time between Virginia and Maine. *Posh Celebrations* is their first book.

Posh Celebrations

Written by Susan Rogers

with Posh Rogers

Illustrated by Carole Pivarnik

PROPERLY POSH PUBLICATIONS

ISBN 978-0-9970720-4-4

Published by
Properly Posh Publications
PO Box 1466
Middleburg, Virginia 20118
202.492.3593

Properly Posh Publications is an imprint of
Properly Posh Pets, LLC.

First Paperback Edition 2016

Book design, layout, and illustrations by Carole Pivarnik.

Table of Contents

P

POSH TALK

Why did I decide to write a party book?

I've been giving fun and memorable parties for years at a variety of locations and for a variety of events – and with the encouragement of family and friends, I decided to share my expertise and secrets to giving successful parties. I specialize in parties that are sophisticated – but whimsical.

Great parties have magical elements, and I am very, very good at developing the vision for parties that create unforgettable moments. I love to socialize and share with all of my family and friends – and parties give me a reason to create amazing gift bags, serve distinctive Classic Cocktails, and prepare delicious food.

But most of all, I love being the STAR of the party, so I thought it might be an excellent idea to write a book that tells lots of other dogs and cats – and their humans – how to recreate the fantastic parties I have become so well known for in my circle of friends.

I hope you will use my ideas, smile at my thoughts, delight in the illustrations – and create your own fabulous, magical parties to celebrate your special furry family and friends.

Go confidently in the direction of your dreams. Give the party you have imagined.

- Posh Proverb

1 Paws to Celebrate!

Paws to Remember: The key to a magical party is the laughter and the friendship and the memories you'll have long after the party is over.

But first, we have to plan the party – and that is why you need this book!

Successful parties require several elements – but Posh knows that they start with a vision and a theme, and he is in charge of that task. Next comes the planning and organization, and he knows that I am the expert at that kind of work, so he has delegated the details in this book to me.

These parties are designed to be an invitation to connect with friends, have fun, and celebrate your pets. The secret to giving a fun and memorable party is planning, organization, and creative ideas – and that's how this book can help you. We cover the basics of parties with information on how to include your pet in the planning and the festivities – and the memories.

You can follow all of the ideas in each party, combine elements from different parties, or use our ideas for inspiration. Posh designed this book as a guide for the busy person who loves to give parties and loves their pets, but doesn't want to work like a dog in order to throw a fabulous party!

This chapter will explain how to use the book to create your theme and develop it through the party planning process from beginning to end. It covers "setting the scene" details including location, theme, invitations, decorations, tableware, and music. We also offer suggestions for celebrating your pet at the party, creating memorable gift bags for your guests, and planning your cocktails and menu.

CHEF
CUDDY

Then you can decide which of the themed parties laid out in the book will be your first "Paws to Celebrate Your Pet" party! Posh has been advising me on how to throw parties in his honor for years – and he selected his seven favorite parties for this inaugural *Posh Celebrations* party guide.

The Posh's Party Recipes chapter includes several recipes from the party menus with ideas on how to vary the recipe for different parties. The Posh's Party Resources chapter includes lists of sources you can use for decoration, gift, and food ideas found in the book.

CHEEKY CHATTER

Throughout the book, you will see that Posh's favorite feline friends Alessandra (aka Ali) and Zhivago (aka Z) have contributed their ideas and thoughts to his party guide. Look for Ali's Cheeky Chatter and Z's Terrific Tip icons.

If you give parties on a regular basis, decide what part of the party is your favorite and make that your "signature" element for every party you throw. Posh loves to design a fabulous party gift bag while my favorite task is selecting the Classic Cocktail.

TERRIFIC TIP

One organizational tip is to prepare a standard party checklist that covers how to prepare your house, food, pets, dishes, decorations etc. Posh asked me to include a sample of our list in Chapter 10, Posh's Party Resources.

Set the Scene

Theme

Your first decision is to pick a theme for your party – and consider whether you are going to be celebrating a special event in the life of your pet, such as a birthday or an adoption. The ideas in this book can be combined so you may decide to celebrate your pet's birthday by hosting a vineyard party. Pick your theme to fit an event, a location, or the season of the year.

Location

This book includes themed parties that can be held at a number of locations including your home, dog-friendly restaurants (such as on the patio), a vineyard, the beach, or a rented space. Some themes work well in moving the party outside, such as "Life's a Beach!".

Guests

People are the element that make your party fun so invite good friends, but always mix in some new and different people. When compiling your guest list, don't forget to include your friends who are dog and cat lovers, but who are not pet owners.

Color Scheme

Pick a color scheme based on your theme with two to three colors, which you can then use for your decorations, tableware, gift bags, menu, and even your Classic Cocktail.

Invitations

Every great party – and every great party theme – begins with the invitation. Your invitations should be personalized, but easy and fun to do. They will set the tone for your party and provide the guests with details they need.

For Posh's themed parties, he believes that written invitations are essential, and the options for doing them include traditional fill-in-the-blank invitations, written information on a postcard or note card, and custom-printed invitations you make at home, order from an online company, or buy from your local stationery store.

Calling All
VINO DOGS
and their
HUMANS
Tasting
EAT
DRINK
BE SCARY
PLEASE JOIN US FOR A
KITTEN
SHOWER
FREE
KISS
AHOY
POSH
INVITES YOU TO
COME SAIL
WITH HIM
for a
CELEBRATION
DINNER
Saturday
July 12
530 pm
KENNEBUNKPORT
marina
rsvp posh@properlyposhpets.com

Here are some ideas for personalizing your invitations:

- Find prepackaged invitations in your party colors and personalize them with stickers from the party theme and photos of your pet, or order custom stickers of your pet. You will be able to write the details of your party on the invitation, and you can be creative with your wording to highlight the party theme and refer to your pet. Include a favorite quote about dogs or cats, such as "There are no ordinary cats."
- For one party, Posh custom ordered his invitation as a bookmark with the announcement of a new feline brother including a picture and details about the adoption party.
- Use notecards with pictures of scenes or objects related to the party theme and include details of your party with a picture of your pet.
- If you feel your pet has too many toys already, include "No Presents Please" on your invitation.
- Make it clear in your invitation whether your friends are being invited to bring their pets with them. Include "Dogs Are Welcome" on your invite!

Decorations

Posh knows that there are lots of very creative party givers who are good at making their own decorations – and he also knows that I am not one of those people, so you will find several sources for buying customizable decorations in Chapter 10.

- Balloons are an easy, economical decoration that can match any party theme or you can use pawprint balloons for any of your parties.
- Mini-string lights are a low-cost way to decorate for all parties – you can coordinate the color of the lights to your party theme colors.
- Decorate with large pictures or posters of your pet and personalized banners, such as "Happy Birthday, Posh."
- Candles are an inexpensive way to make a party festive, but because you will have furry guests at the party, always make sure that any candles are out of reach of tails!

Tableware

Current versions of melamine dishes look great and are durable and affordable, especially if you buy colors that can be used for a variety of themed parties. You can then add napkins and tablecloths that complement your theme and your party colors.

Music

Music helps to set the tone and mood of your party. Your playlist can relate to the theme of the party or your pet – or both! Challenge your guests to add to your playlist ideas to match the theme.

Celebrate Your Pet

Order custom stickers of your pet and use them to decorate invitations, notepads and gift bags – and pretty much anything else that relates to your party!

LET'S
PARTY
Boomer

Pet Attire and Costumes

Dress your pet to coordinate with your party theme and color scheme – ranging from a "Birthday Boy" bandana, to a sweater for the "Touchdown!" party, to a full-out pirate costume for the "Tricks for Treats" party.

Pet Gifts

The ideas we have included for pet gifts can be used to shower your own pet with presents as the guest of honor or provide ideas for gifts to include in your party gift bags that will go home with your guests for their pets.

If the party is the type of event where guests would bring gifts for your pet, set up a gift registry with an online retailer to give your guests gift ideas, such as for the "Welcome to the Family" party. Include a link to the "wish list" on your invitation.

You may also want to give your guests the option of donating to an animal rescue group in honor of your pet. Your local rescue group will have a "wish list" that you can provide your guests if you want to collect gifts or donations for their animals.

KISSING BOOTH
PLAYLIST
To do:
Find songs that go with my party theme!
- Search online
- Check my DVDs

Entertainment

The music you pick may be all the entertainment you need – but by making your pet the center of attention at your party, you will find that there are lots of fun ideas for additional entertainment to complement the theme or the event being celebrated at the party.

- Incorporate a photo booth in your party to give your guests a chance to interact with your pet and create "forever memories." Designate a spot in the party area where the photos can be taken and provide a neutral backdrop and fun props that match the party's theme, such as a giant red heart for "Be Mine, Valentine."
- Plan for contests that coordinate with your party theme – for example, the "Tricks for Treats" party should include costume contests, and the vineyard party is a perfect opportunity to compete for "Best Vino Dog" and "Best Trick."
- Invite an artist or photographer – maybe a friend with a hobby – to your party to help capture the party memories.
- Include an activity that relates to your party theme, such as a winery tour at the vineyard party or a touch football game at the "Touchdown" party.

Although these parties are designed so that your pet may be the only four-legged guest in attendance, you need to be conscious of safety precautions for your pet and any four-legged guests who join in the fun. Include pet-friendly food items including healthy dog treats.

Posh loves getting gifts – but he really loves giving them, and at the very first party he gave, he insisted that he wanted his guests to take home some tangible memories from his party. And the gift bags have become more and more elaborate over the years – so much so that friends have told him they are one of the highlights of his parties!

Decorating your Gift Bag

- Use solid colored paper mini-shopping bags matching your party's colors and coordinated tissue.
- Add custom stickers of your pet and stickers that coordinate with your party theme, such as hearts for "Be Mine, Valentine."
- Tie the bag handles with coordinated ribbon, pawprint ribbon, or personalized ribbon with your pet's name. Attach a small ornament or toy, such as a sailboat for "Life's a Beach!".
- Wrap individual items - such as Posh's Party Cookies - in small cellophane bags with ribbon.

Contents of your Gift Bag

- Coordinate the contents with your party theme.
- Include the ingredients for your party's Classic Cocktail using liquor miniatures and the classic glass used for your cocktail, such as a champagne flute for Posh's Blue Champagne Cocktail. Put the miniatures and the glass in small cellophane bags. Print the recipe for your Classic Cocktail on a color-coordinated notecard and staple to the ingredients bag. Put two cocktail napkins in a cellophane bag tied with ribbon or a swizzle stick that matches the party theme. Custom order cocktail napkins with your Classic Cocktail recipe. Include printed recipes for cocktails related to your Classic Cocktail.
- Posh has a signature party cookie (Posh's Party Cookies in Chapter 9), which he always includes with the cookies cut in shapes that match the party theme, such as hearts for "Be Mine, Valentine." Wrap two cookies in a cellophane bag tied with ribbon. Include a cookie cutter related to the party theme, such as a heart or sailboat.
- Include small boxes of candy matching the party theme or wrap candy in small cellophane bags. Posh made truffles one year for the "Be Mine, Valentine" party and sent two truffles home with every guest.
- Tiny books are always a good gift bag idea – such as pet books or books about friends.

- Ornaments that match the party theme are a cute memento – one year for Nick's "Make a Wish" party, Posh bought Cheshire Cat ornaments reflecting Nick's mischievous personality.
- Personalize items like matches, notepads, and cocktail napkins with your pet's name, picture, or cute quotes.
- Include mini pet calendars and mini stuffed animals to complement your theme.
- Select food items that coordinate with your theme, such as microwave popcorn or candy bars.
- Choose CDs or DVDs to fit your party theme.

Create the Classic Cocktail

Select a "signature cocktail" for your party that relates to the party theme or your pet. You can serve the Classic Cocktail at your party and include the ingredients in your Gift Bag so that your guests can make the drink at home – and remember how much fun your party was!

Tie your Classic Cocktail to something personal, such as your pet's name or an experience you have shared. You can find a drink that includes the name of your pet or rename a classic cocktail to include your pet's name. For example, to celebrate a dog named Brandy, serve a Brandy Alexander.

Plan Your Menu

When you plan your menu, think about recipes and food that you can prepare before the party so you aren't stuck in the kitchen missing all the fun. Keep your menu simple with one custom recipe that will make your food memorable. Consider having printed menus and setting a small place card in front of food items to identify them. Always make more than enough food so you don't have to worry about running out. Try to include a variety of food in the event you have guests with dietary restrictions.

Fun Food Feature

- Incorporating a food or drink bar in your party is a way to add a creative food-related activity to your party. This is also a good way to incorporate your party's theme and colors into the decorations. Plan a cupcake bar or a sundae bar.
- Consider having a contest to vote for the best cupcake or sundae – most people love to compete when it comes to creativity.

Post-Party Items

- If your guests brought presents for your pet to the party, don't forget to make sure a thank-you is sent – and make it easy by buying a general thank-you card and personalizing it with a sticker of your pet. Or compose an email to all attendees with a photo from the party from your pet saying "Thanks!".
- Make notes of what worked at your party and what didn't, so that you can use the experience for future parties.
- Create a special memento of your party with an online photo album using pictures from the party of your pet and your guests with cute captions.

Let's Get This Party Started!

Posh has given you the roadmap to celebrating with your friends and furry family, and now he will share some of his secrets to his favorite themed parties. Pick your theme, draft your guest list, send your invitations, create your classic cocktail, plan your menu, and start your shopping for party attire, food, and gift bag items.

But always Paws to Remember: The fun of parties is planning, anticipating, enjoying, and remembering!

POSH TALK

For several years on Valentine's Day, I hosted a birthday party for my brother Nick who had the bad luck to be born the day after Christmas when no one wants to come to a party. Since Valentine’s Day is one of my favorite holidays, it seemed the perfect excuse to throw a party and celebrate my feline friend. With a reputation for being a bit of a "grumbly" cat, Nick found himself surrounded by hearts and kisses and hugs from a distance!

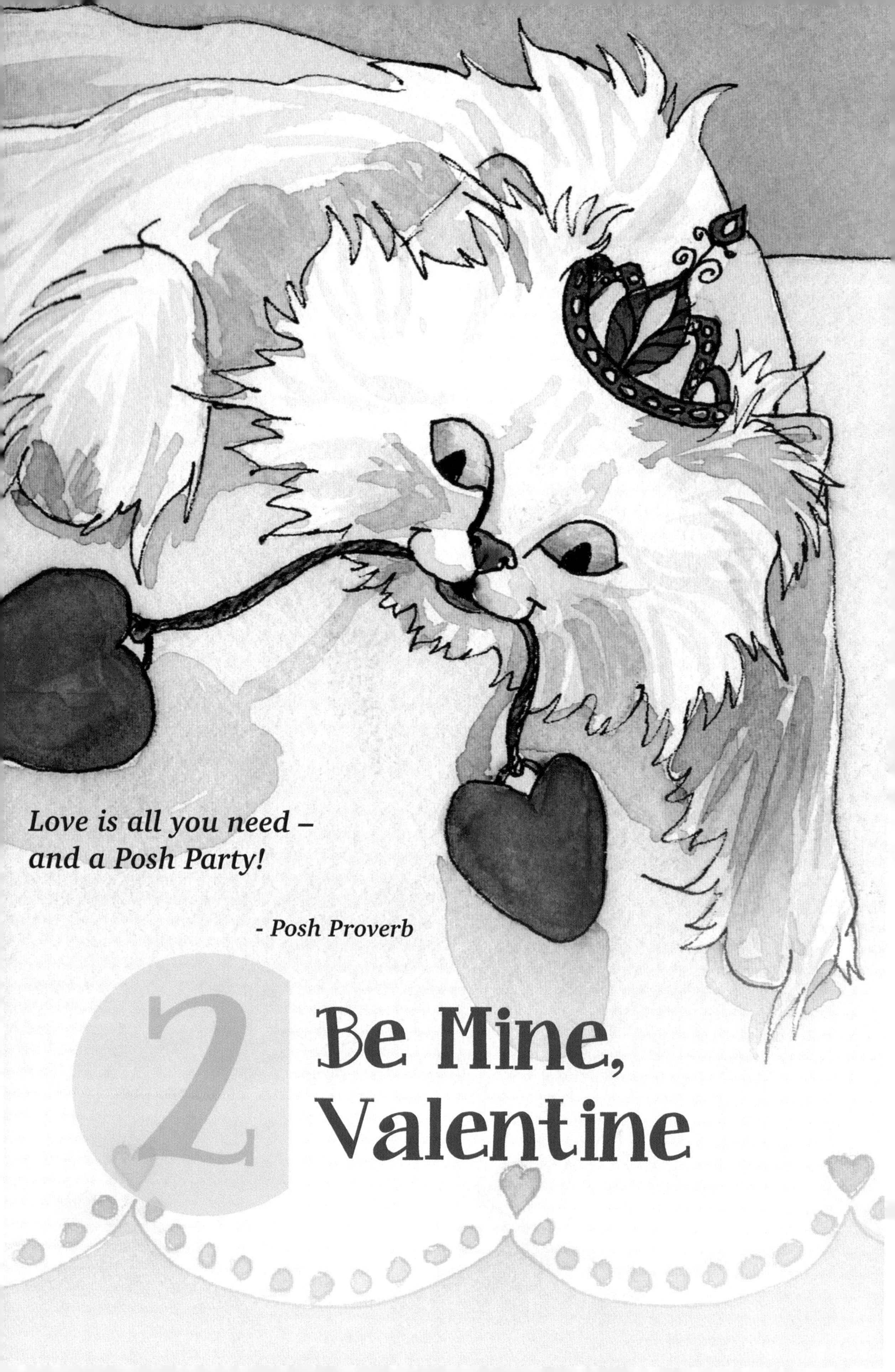

Love is all you need –
and a Posh Party!

- Posh Proverb

2 Be Mine, Valentine

Set the Scene

Plan to host a Valentine's Day brunch at home to create a festive break from winter – and an excuse to decorate your house with cheerful red, pink, and purple hearts in all shapes and sizes.

Use a "conversation hearts" theme – fill bowls with the nostalgic candy, provide blank paper hearts for guests to write their own messages, and hang streamers of paper "conversation hearts" with personalized messages, using classic sayings such as "True Love" and "Be Mine," mixed with current sayings such as "Text Me" and "Cool Dude."

TERRIFIC TIP

Search online for lists of conversation heart sayings and include emoji ideas.

FREE KISS
NICK INVITES YOU
to be
HIS VALENTINE
at a brunch on
SATURDAY, FEBRUARY the 14th
at 11:30 a.m.
RSVP
posh@properlyposhpets.com
FREE KISS

String white, red, and pink mini-string lights for sparkle and to set the scene for romance.

Drape heart garlands around centerpieces, mantels, and door frames.

Print the Classic Cocktail recipe on custom napkins with a heart graphic.

Order matchbooks customized with your Pet of Honor's name and a heart graphic.

Order "Hugs from" notepads customized with your Pet of Honor's name.

Love is in the Air Playlist

Stop! In the Name of Love - The Supremes

Someone Like You - Adele

I Finally Found Someone - Barbra Streisand

I Left My Heart in San Francisco - Tony Bennett

Hopeless Romantic - Meghan Trainor

I Will Always Love You - Whitney Houston

Fly Me to the Moon - Frank Sinatra

Crazy - Patsy Cline

Will You Love Me Tomorrow - Carole King

KISSING
BOOTH

Use a giant red heart as a backdrop for candid pictures of your Pet of Honor and his guests claiming their Free Kisses.

TERRIFIC TIP

If your Cat of Honor resists wearing his cute red collar, promise him a shrimp or other special treat!

NICK

Gifts for Nick

- Heart or mouse toys
- Treats
- Feather wand toy

BE
MINE
AMORE

Gift Bag Decoration

- Use a white or pink bag.
- Go wild with heart and pet stickers.
- Tie with pink, red, and purple ribbon.
- Use purple, red, and pink tissue paper.

Gifts for Nick's Guests

- Mini box of chocolates
- Homemade truffles
- Conversation hearts
- Wine glass charms
- Romantic movie DVD
- Love songs CD
- Posh's Party Cookies (heart-shaped)

Classic Cocktail Mini-Bag

- Amaretto miniature
- Frangelico miniature
- 2 liqueur glasses
- 2 cocktail napkins
- Printed recipe for "The Poshiano"

Create the Classic Cocktail

1 ounce of Amaretto
1 ounce of Frangelico

The Poshiano

Mix the Amaretto and Frangelico together. Serve in a liqueur glass.

CHEEKY CHATTER

Posh, the Canine Mixologist, concocted this special drink for Nick's party but named it after himself!

Brunch Menu

- Rogers Chicken Casserole
- Quiche Lorraine and spinach quiche
- Shrimp salad
- Sliced melon and strawberries
- Whipped cream fruit salad
- Scones
- Parmesan biscuits
- Cinnamon rolls
- Cranberry juice spritzers and sparkling wine
- Posh's Party Cake

TERRIFIC TIP

Posh's Party Cake is an angel food cake with whipped cream frosting. Use a heart-shaped pan or create mini cakes by using individual cake pans. I hid the secret recipe in Chapter 9!

Posh's Chocolate Bar

- Chocolate-dipped strawberries
- Posh's Magical Fudge in heart-shaped mini-pans
- Homemade truffles
- Chocolate mousse with whipped cream
- Chocolate Fondue

DR. POSH'S
CUP CAKE
LAB

POSH TALK

Over the past ten years, my annual Posh Birthday Party has become legendary with many of them having taken place at the vineyard owned by my fabulous friends, Holli and John. Having reached a milestone birthday last year, I have now decided to stop counting the years and will be "forever 10" for each amazing party yet to come! I love being the center of attention but PLEASE don't make me wear the party hat. I have picked my favorite party from past years for you to recreate at your house to celebrate one more year of fun and laughter with your favorite furry friend.

Every dog must have his POSH Party Birthday!

- Posh Proverb

3 Make a Wish!

Set the Scene

Posh picked balloons as the theme for his birthday bash. Balloons are a simple, colorful addition to your party designed to create a festive mood.

TERRIFIC TIP

Include "no presents please" if you think your Pet of Honor has too many toys or suggest a donation to your local animal rescue group.

HAPPY BIRTHDAY POSH
IDICULOUSLY CUTE
IT'S EXHAUSTING BEING ABULOUS
ROCK STAR
I'M KIND OF A BIG DEAL AROUND HERE!
IT'S ALL ABOUT ME!!!

PLEASE JOIN ME on SATURDAY, SEPT 17th 2 to 5 PM to
PAWS and CELEBRATE POSH
on his 10th BIRTHDAY!
Place: Posh's House
RSVP: susan@properlyposhpets.com

Fill your house with colorful pawprint balloons. Form your Pet of Honor's name and age with balloons taped to the wall.

Use "Dog" or "Cat" themed birthday decorations, which can be found online.

Find a "bone piñata" and fill it with tiny packages of dog treats for guests to take home to their dogs.

Custom order cocktail napkins with "Posh is 10."

Freeze water tinted with food coloring in number-shaped trays for the age of your Pet of Honor for use in your guests' drinks.

TERRIFIC TIP

Pick songs with titles that include "party," "celebration," and "birthday," and don't forget to include the dance music that Posh loves!

Birthday Bash Playlist

Celebration – Kool and the Gang

Birthday – The Beatles

Party in the USA – Miley Cyrus

It's My Party – Lesley Gore

Born to be Wild – Steppenwolf

16 Candles – The Crests

Happy, Happy Birthday, Baby – The Tuneweavers

Happy Birthday, Sweet Sixteen – Neil Sedaka

Born in the USA – Bruce Springsteen

and

Happy Birthday, of course!

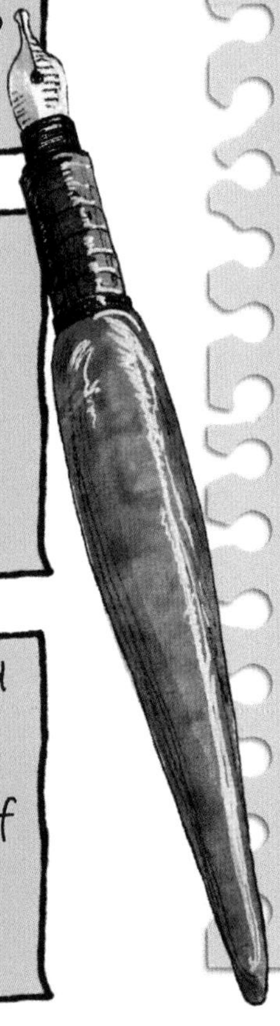

Celebrate Your Pet

A caricature artist will make your birthday bash a blast! Caricaturists are wonderful artists who create customized cartoon drawings in a matter of minutes of your guests – paired with your Pet of Honor. Typically, the artist will ask each person a few things about themselves and then incorporate that into the drawing so that your guests have a fun memento of the party.

Have your Pet of Honor "pawtograph" each cartoon for your guests for a special personal touch.

Set up a corner of the party space with two chairs and a pet bed. Your guests can join in the fun of watching the artist at work.

Gifts for Posh

Outfit Posh with a new wardrobe of bandanas!

- Best Dog
- Best Dog Ever
- Birthday Boy
- Dog of Honor
- Party Animal
- Party Pooch

BEST
FRIENDS

Gift Bag Decoration

Your pet is the STAR of this party, so the bag should be all about him!

- Decorate a blue or red bag with pictures of your “Star” and custom stickers.
- Add balloon and star stickers.
- Tie with red and blue ribbon.

Gifts for Posh’s Guests

Remember the party is all about your Pet of Honor!

- Notepads, mugs, magnets, and mousepads with your pet’s picture
- Dog/cat ornaments
- Small pocket book with a “best friends” theme
- Posh’s Party Cookies (dog- or bone-shaped)

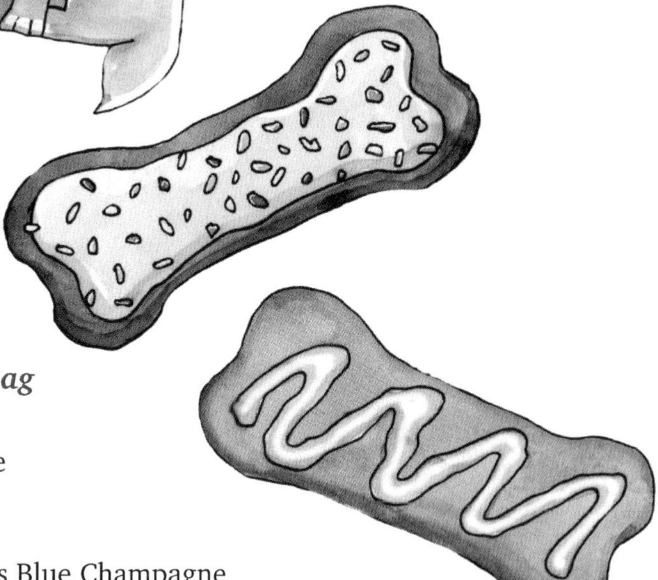

Classic Cocktail Mini-Bag

- Blue Curacao miniature
- Mini-split of Champagne
- 2 champagne flutes
- 2 cocktail napkins
- Printed recipe for "Posh’s Blue Champagne Cocktail"

Also include printed recipes for other Champagne cocktails such as Mimosa, Kir Royale, Bellini, Black Velvet, and French 75.

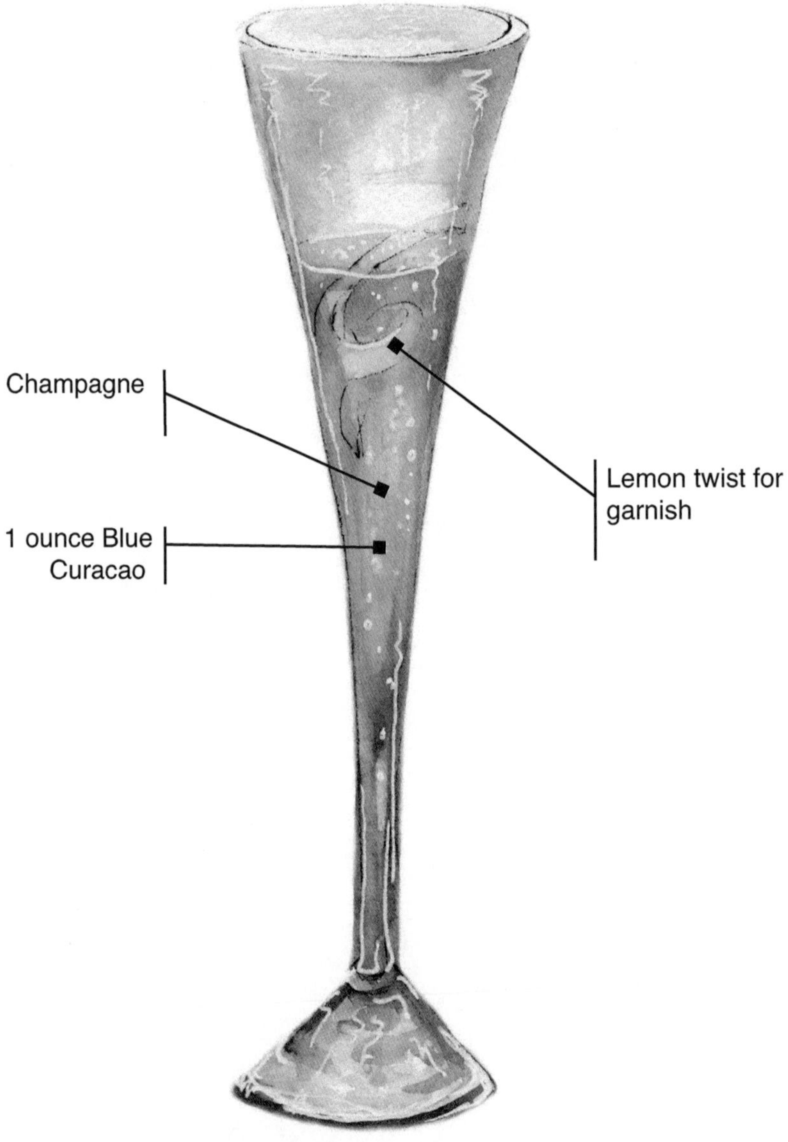
Champagne
1 ounce Blue Curacao
Lemon twist for garnish

Posh's Blue Champagne Cocktail

Fill a champagne flute with Champagne about three quarters full. Add the Blue Curacao. Garnish with a lemon twist.

CHEEKY CHATTER

My favorite sparkling wine is prosecco – so I always use that for my Champagne cocktails as an economical substitute for Champagne.

Birthday Bash Menu

- Posh's Party Dips: Warm Crab Dip and Posh's Baked Feta
- Jumbo shrimp cocktail with cocktail sauce
- Parmesan and herb biscuits
- Glazed ham
- Mac and cheese
- Roasted asparagus with lemon aioli

Posh's Birthday Cake

Use a bone-shaped pan with dog bone candles or balloon candles. Arrange the candles as a number for the age of your Pet of Honor.

CHEEKY CHATTER

Posh has a signature birthday cake for his parties: yellow butter cake with caramel frosting. I put the secret recipe in Chapter 9!

Posh's Sundae Bar

Posh always serves ice cream at his parties, but he makes sure he has dog-safe frosty treats for the four-legged guests.

- Ice cream: vanilla and chocolate
- Sauces: Chocolate, hot fudge, caramel, butterscotch, berry
- Crunchy toppings: Nuts, toffee bits
- Sweet toppings: Chocolate chips, sprinkles, cookie or candy pieces
- Healthy toppings: Berries, cherries, toasted coconut flakes, bananas
- Ali recommends homemade whipped cream in a large bowl with a big spoon.

POSH TALK

My friend John told me that a popular but disputed explanation of the origin of the word "posh" is nautical. As the story goes, "Port Out, Starboard Home" denoted the cooler side of ships traveling from England to India and back again in the 1800s where the cabins were more expensive and given to first class passengers.

I have found my first class "cabin" in Maine at the marina where I watch the boats from the deck of a magical cottage by the sea and visit with Cuddy and Cathy who "captain" the marina.

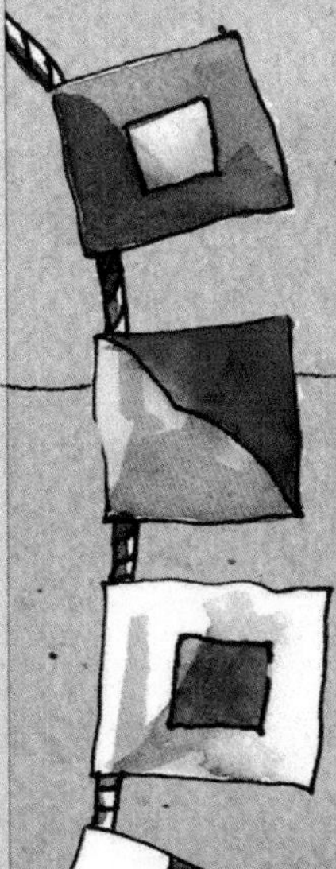

The only thing required for parties to happen is for party animals to hit the beach.

- Posh Proverb

4 Life's a Beach!

Set the Scene

Create a magical cottage by the sea at your home. Posh also suggests the beach, the local marina, a beach house or a boat! Use signs or displays featuring beach sayings or keywords to help create a beach state of mind:

- Party Like a Pirate
- Wake Up Smiling
- Enjoy the Ocean Breeze
- Make a Splash
- Dig for Treasures
- Wish on a Starfish
- Take a Nap
- Seas the Day

Posh's BEACH RULES
BUILD SANDCASTLES
Catch the Waves
SOAK UP THE
be happy as a clam
HAVE FUN
Watch SUNSETS

AHOY
POSH
INVITES YOU TO COME SAIL WITH HIM for a CELEBRATION DINNER
Saturday July 12 5:30 pm
KENNEBUNKPORT marina
rsvp posh@properlyposh
RED WINE
WHITE WINE

Decorate with anchor and boat ornaments, toy lobsters, starfish and other sea creatures, stars, and wooden boats.

Spell out your Pet of Honor's name in nautical flags.

Use wooden signs with beach quotes which are easy to find in beach town stores or online.

Use notecards with pictures of the beach or your favorite seaside town.

Decorate with votive candles with ocean/beach scents in glass bowls surrounded by sea glass.

Sun & Sand Playlist

Beach Boys
- Good Vibrations
- Surfin Safari
- Fun, fun, fun

Jimmy Buffet
- Margaritaville
- Cheeseburgers in Paradise
- Son of a Sailor
- It's Five O'clock Somewhere

The Tide is High – Blondie

Under the Boardwalk – The Drifters

Glory Days – Bruce Springsteen

Joy to the World – Three Dog Night

Brandy, You're a Fine Girl – Looking Glass

Celebrate Your Pet

Karaoke is oh so corny, but oh so popular – and your beach party is a perfect fit for this activity with our Sun and Sand Playlist that invites lots of enthusiastic singing – and if your pet is anything like Posh, he will love joining in by "howling" and dancing! Buy or rent karaoke equipment and set it up in a corner of the party space.

Include all of our suggested tunes from the Sun and Sand Playlist but make sure that you have lots of options available for those who want to perform. It's easy to go online and search for lists of karaoke songs that will get all of your guests in the mood to join in either by grabbing the mike themselves or chiming in from the audience.

Gifts for Remy

- Beach or ocean-themed dog biscuits
- Lobster, anchor, starfish, or whale toys
- Dog bow ties with anchors or lobsters
- "Crab" dog hat
- Bandanas with anchors, lobsters, seahorses, or seashells

CAPTAIN
REMY

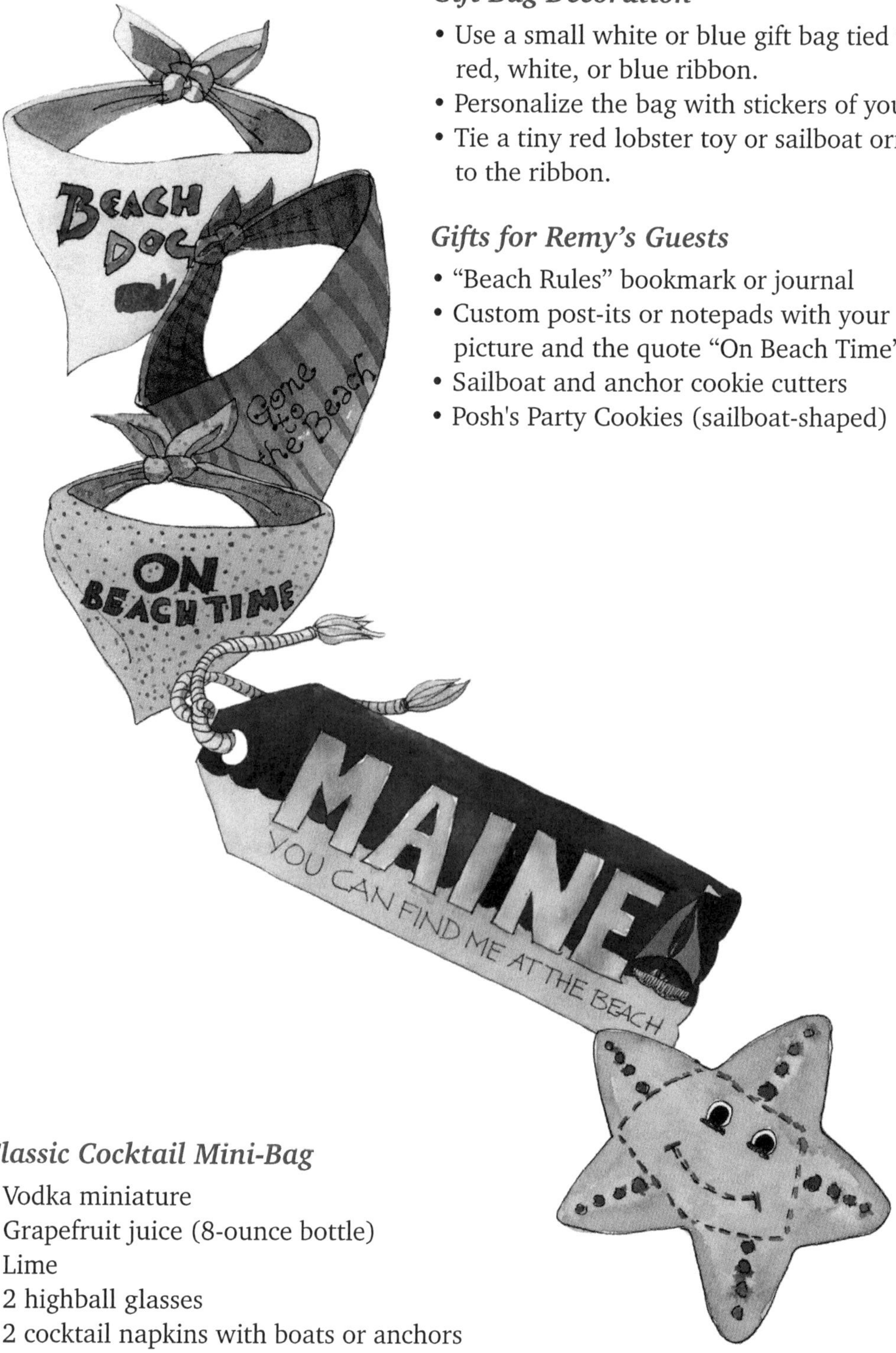
BEACH DOG
Gone to the Beach
ON BEACH TIME
MAINE
YOU CAN FIND ME AT THE BEACH

Gift Bag Decoration

- Use a small white or blue gift bag tied with red, white, or blue ribbon.
- Personalize the bag with stickers of your pet.
- Tie a tiny red lobster toy or sailboat ornament to the ribbon.

Gifts for Remy's Guests

- "Beach Rules" bookmark or journal
- Custom post-its or notepads with your pet's picture and the quote "On Beach Time"
- Sailboat and anchor cookie cutters
- Posh's Party Cookies (sailboat-shaped)

Classic Cocktail Mini-Bag

- Vodka miniature
- Grapefruit juice (8-ounce bottle)
- Lime
- 2 highball glasses
- 2 cocktail napkins with boats or anchors
- Swizzle stick with anchor or lobster
- Printed recipe for "The Salty Dog"

Create the Classic Cocktail

Garnish with lime slices, lime juice, and coarse kosher salt
½ ounce fresh lime juice
1½ ounces vodka
¾ cup fresh ruby red grapefruit juice

The Salty Dog

Dip rim of highball glass into lime juice, then into kosher salt to coat. Fill a cocktail shaker halfway with ice. Add grapefruit juice, lime juice, and vodka. Shake vigorously for 5 to 10 seconds. Strain over ice into prepared glass. Garnish with lime slices.

CHEEKY CHATTER

The term "salty dog" is nautical slang for an experienced sailor. Posh, I don't think sitting on the deck at the marina in Kennebunkport qualifies you as an "experienced sailor." Get yourself a boat!

Beach Menu

- Posh's Clam Chowder with oyster crackers
- Boiled shrimp with cocktail sauce
- Lobster rolls or lobster mac and cheese
- Mini-crab cakes with remoulade sauce
- Corn on the cob, corn casserole or cornbread
- Sliced fresh tomatoes with basil and vinaigrette
- Key lime pie and blueberry pie
- Whoopie Pies and "Woofie Pies"

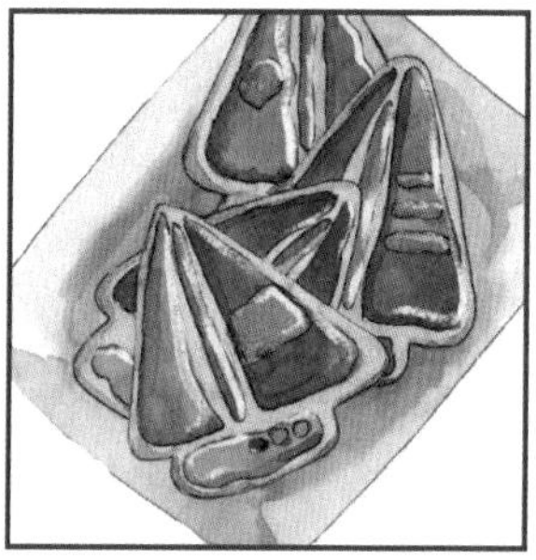

CHEEKY CHATTER

The Woofie Pie is called the official Maine treat for dogs. It is two whole wheat carob biscuits with a filling of yogurt.

Posh's Beer Bar

- Visit your local craft brewery for growlers filled with classic and unusual beers, ales, IPAs, and lagers.
- Mix beer cocktails such as the Black and Tan, the Black Velvet, and the Shandy.
- Serve beers with nautical names.
- Create custom beer bottle labels with pictures of your Pet of Honor or add your pet picture sticker to the bottle or growler.

TERRIFIC TIP

A “growler” is a container used for the transport of draft beer – not my sister Ali when she’s having a bad day!

POSH TALK

I threw an adoption party on August 2, 2014, to welcome Alessandra and Zhivago to my world. According to the petiquette experts, it was ok for me to throw a kitten shower to honor my new furry friends even though I am family. Ali and Z helped me with lots of ideas for the party, so I have graciously allowed them to be the STARS of this chapter.

I scheduled the party for early evening so that the Kittens of Honor wouldn't fall asleep in the middle of the party. Because they were meeting my friends for the first time, I wanted to make sure that they were relaxed and ready for fun at the party, so I decorated the sunroom as their personal party space where they could be gated with their toys and beds with plenty of room for the party guests to meet and greet them. Midway through the party, Ali went wild playing with her shower presents – too much catnip, I guess!

IT'S A
GIRL

Kittens are kisses blown to us by fairies.

- Posh Proverb

5 Welcome to the Family

Set the Scene

Plan your "kitten debut" party for home to ensure that they are relaxed and have fun at the party. Posh decided to add a Russian theme to his "sip and see" party so that the party guests would remember Zhivago's name!

Posh set up a "Kitten Wish List" for Ali and Z on the website of a national online retailer and included a link to it on the invitation. Z asked for the laser toys, but Ali was happy with the tiny yellow mouse from her Aunt Holli.

ALI's
ADOPTION RULES
KISS ME, HUG ME, LOVE ME, ADOPT ME
SINGLE FURRY FRIEND ISO FOREVER FAMILY
PSST... I'M AVAILABLE!
LOVE IS JUST A CAT AWAY
OOH! OOH! PICK ME!
PLEASE JOIN US FOR A
KITTEN SHOWER
IN HONOR OF
ALESSANDRA
and
ZHIVAGO
SUSAN & POSH'S SILVER-SHADED PERSIAN KITTENS HAVE ARRIVED!
SATURDAY
AUGUST 2
5 PM AT POSH'S PLACE
RSVP
posh@properlyposhpets.com

TERRIFIC TIP

Consider inviting your vet in recognition of the important part they will play in the life of your new kittens.

Posh decided the cutest party decorations would be Ali and Z so he focused his time and money on party gift bags.

Order large prints of your new kittens as babies.

Posh ordered custom silver napkins with the party drink "Ali and Z's Cocktail" in a purple font.

Buy blue and pink party mints with "Baby Girl" and "Baby Boy" and put in bowls around the party area.

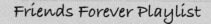

Friends Forever Playlist

Baby Love – The Supremes

With a Little Help from My Friends – The Beatles

Count on Me – Bruno Mars

Home – Phillip Phillips

Can't Take My Eyes Off of You – Franki Valli and the Four Seasons

That's What Friends are For – Dionne Warwick

Wannabe (Friendship never ends) – The Spice Girls

Friends in Low Places – Garth Brooks

You're My Best Friend – Queen

Rescue Me – Aretha Franklin

CHEEKY CHATTER

Posh found a purple wooden sign that reads "It's All About Me" – so perfect for a party where I am the star!

"Kitten Photo Booth" and Party Games

- Snap pictures of the party guests with the "Kittens of Honor."
- Make sure you get a group picture and lots of "action shots" as this party will be a memorable event for you and your new furry family members.
- Have guests guess the weight of each of the kittens and award a prize for the closest guess.
- Create a special memento for yourself at one of the online photo/printing companies by using a collection of photos taken at the party and personalized with comments about the party, kittens of honor, and guests. Thanks, Aunt Laura, for this idea!

CHEEKY CHATTER

One present came in a purple floral box that Ali used to collect mementos of the party including ribbon from all of the presents, cards, the invitation, the menu, and a cocktail napkin.

Kitten Wish List

- Toys – laser, motion, scratchers, tiny mice
- Treats (for kittens or puppies)
- Photo album
- Blankets
- Empty bags, tissue, and ribbon
- Donation cards for local animal rescue groups

ALI
Z

IT'S A GIRL
IT'S A BOY

Gift Bag Decoration

- Posh used a white bag with pink and purple tissue.
- He decorated the bags with custom stickers of a photo of Ali & Z taken on the first day they arrived, sleeping in their new personalized beds.
- He ordered custom ribbon with "Alessandra" and "Zhivago" to tie on the bag handle.

Gifts for Ali & Z's Guests

- Zhivago's favorite Russian movie DVD
- Mini-bag of microwave popcorn
- Dark chocolate candy bar
- Notepad with Ali & Z photos
- Mini-bags of Baby Boy/Baby Girl mints
- Posh's Party Cookies (kitten-shaped)

POSH
CHOCOLATE
ALI

Z

Classic Cocktail Mini-Bag

- Vodka miniature
- Coffee-flavored liqueur miniature
- 2 old-fashioned glasses
- 2 cocktail napkins
- Printed recipe for "Ali & Z's Cocktail" (aka White Russian)

Create the Classic Cocktail

2 ounces vodka
1 ounce coffee-flavored liqueur
1 cup ice
1 ounce heavy cream

Ali & Z's Cocktail (aka White Russian)

Combine vodka, liqueur, and ice in old-fashioned glass. Pour in cream. Do not stir.

TERRIFIC TIP

You can create a "Russian" using vodka, gin, and Creme de Cacao; a "Black Russian" with vodka and coffee-flavored liqueur; and a "Russian Bear" by mixing vodka, Creme de Cacao, cream, and sugar!

Kitten Shower Menu

- Cheese and crackers
- Shrimp with cocktail sauce
- Mini sandwiches including ham with herb biscuits, brioche with London broil, and mini-croissants with chicken salad
- Sliced fresh tomatoes with basil and vinaigrette
- Potato salad
- Coleslaw
- Deviled eggs
- Strawberries with crème fraiche

CHEEKY CHATTER

Posh is a little sensitive about hearing people say, “He’s a big Westie, isn’t he?” Susan describes him as “sturdy,” but I tease him about being chubby from eating too many cupcakes when he throws a POSH party!

Posh’s Cupcake Bar

Give your guests a fun activity at the party with a cupcake bar that allows them to customize their own cupcakes. Bake two flavors of cupcakes, such as white and chocolate. Make cupcakes in a variety of sizes and use cupcake papers in your party theme colors. Make two flavors of frosting, such as cream cheese and chocolate buttercream.

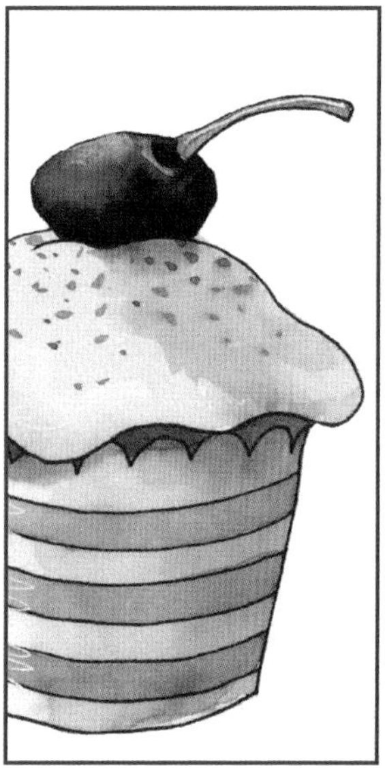

Provide a variety of toppings including: sprinkles and colored glitter sugar (in your party theme colors), dark and white chocolate chips, nuts, coconut, M&M’s, sea salt, mini-marshmallows, Heath bar crumble, and candied fruit pieces.

Let your guests decorate their cupcakes with cake toppers and picks with designs such as cats, dogs, hearts, or baby carriages. My friend Barbie suggests arranging the cupcakes on a cupcake tree that can be customized to match your party colors.

POSH TALK

I was the reigning "Best Virginia Wine Dog" for 2011 and 2012 and the official "Vino Dog" at Three Fox Vineyards in Delaplane, Virginia, where I have helped with all phases of the winery operations from planting the vines through harvesting, bottling, and marketing.

The owners, Holli and John, created a special wine just for me called "Sirius" – with my picture as the DOG STAR on the label.

VINO DOG
SIRIUS

Eat, DRINK, sleep, play, love, PARTY!!!

- Posh Proverb

6 Vines, Wines, Fun Times!

Set the Scene

Many wineries are dog-friendly, so host your party to celebrate your pet at a local winery. Encourage your friends to bring their own dogs.

Plan the party for harvest time in the fall when the grapes are at peak growth. Include a wine tasting and a tour of the winery as part of your "entertainment" and note that on your invitation.

At the party, appoint a "Vino Dog Guardian" to watch your canine guests as they will not be allowed where the winemaking machinery is located.

POSH'S WINE RULES
POUR
SIP
FETCH
STAY
DRINK
CHEER
Calling All VINO DOGS and their HUMANS to a POSH PARTY!
Saturday
September 17
4:00 p.m.
THREE FOX VINEYARDS
Wine Tasting
Winery Tour
Supper
RSVP: posh@properlyposhpets.com

TERRIFIC TIP

Take a picture of your dog in front of the vines or next to a bottle of wine and wine glass to include in your invitation.

Use pawprint balloons to signal the party location at the vineyard.

TERRIFIC TIP

Offer departing guests a balloon as a party memento.

Invite an artist or photographer who specializes in canine art to your party.

Contact your local pet store or arts society for referrals.

Ask a local art group to schedule a "sketch day" on the date of your party.

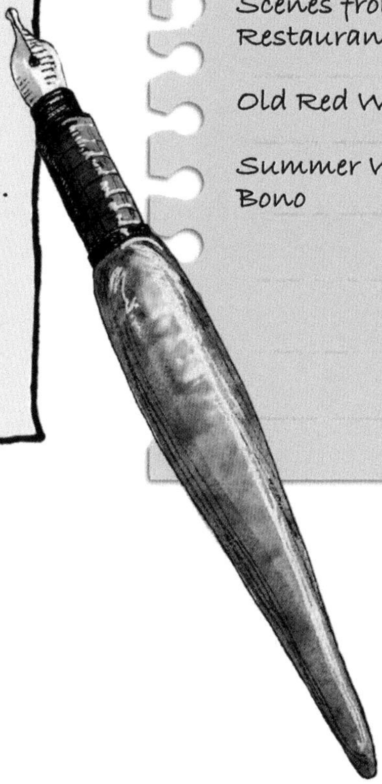

The Wine Dog Playlist

Who Let the Dogs Out – Baha Men

The Puppy Song – Harry Nillson

Puppy Love – Paul Anka

Hound Dog – Elvis Presley

I Love My Dog – Cat Stevens

How Much is that Doggie in the Window – Patti Page

Red, Red Wine – Neil Diamond

Strawberry Wine – Deana Carter

Scenes from an Italian Restaurant – Billy Joel

Old Red Wine – The Who

Summer Wine – Corrs with Bono

Celebrate Your Pet

Dog Contests

Entertain dogs and humans alike with:

- Best Wine Dog – each dog is asked to drink water out of a wine glass held by the owner; give prizes for "Fastest Drinker" and "Funniest Drinker"
- Best Owner/Dog Look-alike
- Best Trick
- Most Stylish
- Best Kisser

TERRIFIC TIP

Fill a giant clear treat jar with dog treats and challenge the humans to guess the number of treats in the jar.

Contest Prizes

- Bandanas
- Wine bottle toys
- Dog treats

Gifts for Rose and Jack

- Custom bandanas with "Wine Dog," "Vino Dog," or "Drinking Buddy"
- Logo bandana from the host winery
- Collar and leash with a wine theme
- Wine bottle toys

ROSE
wine
mascot
JACK
wine
mascot

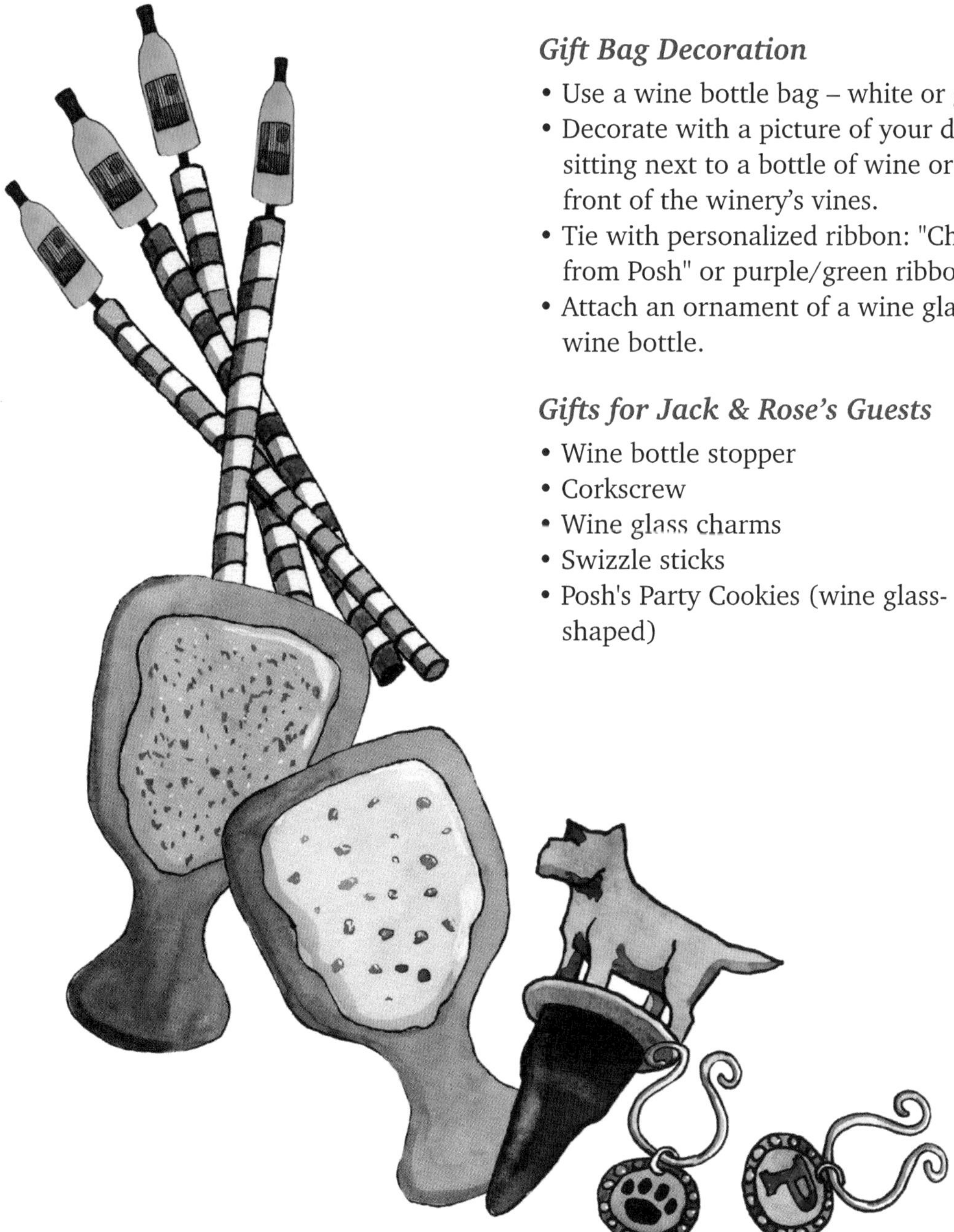

Gift Bag Decoration

- Use a wine bottle bag – white or gold.
- Decorate with a picture of your dog sitting next to a bottle of wine or in front of the winery's vines.
- Tie with personalized ribbon: "Cheers from Posh" or purple/green ribbon.
- Attach an ornament of a wine glass or wine bottle.

Gifts for Jack & Rose's Guests

- Wine bottle stopper
- Corkscrew
- Wine glass charms
- Swizzle sticks
- Posh's Party Cookies (wine glass-shaped)

Classic Cocktail Mini-Bag

- Bottle of red wine
- Triple sec or Cointreau miniature
- Brandy miniature
- 2 wine glasses
- 2 cocktail napkins
- Printed recipe for "Posh's Vineyard Sangria"

TERRIFIC TIP

Ask your host winery to create a custom label with your dog's picture – or put custom stickers on a bottle of wine – your dog's picture and a "Cheers!" sticker.

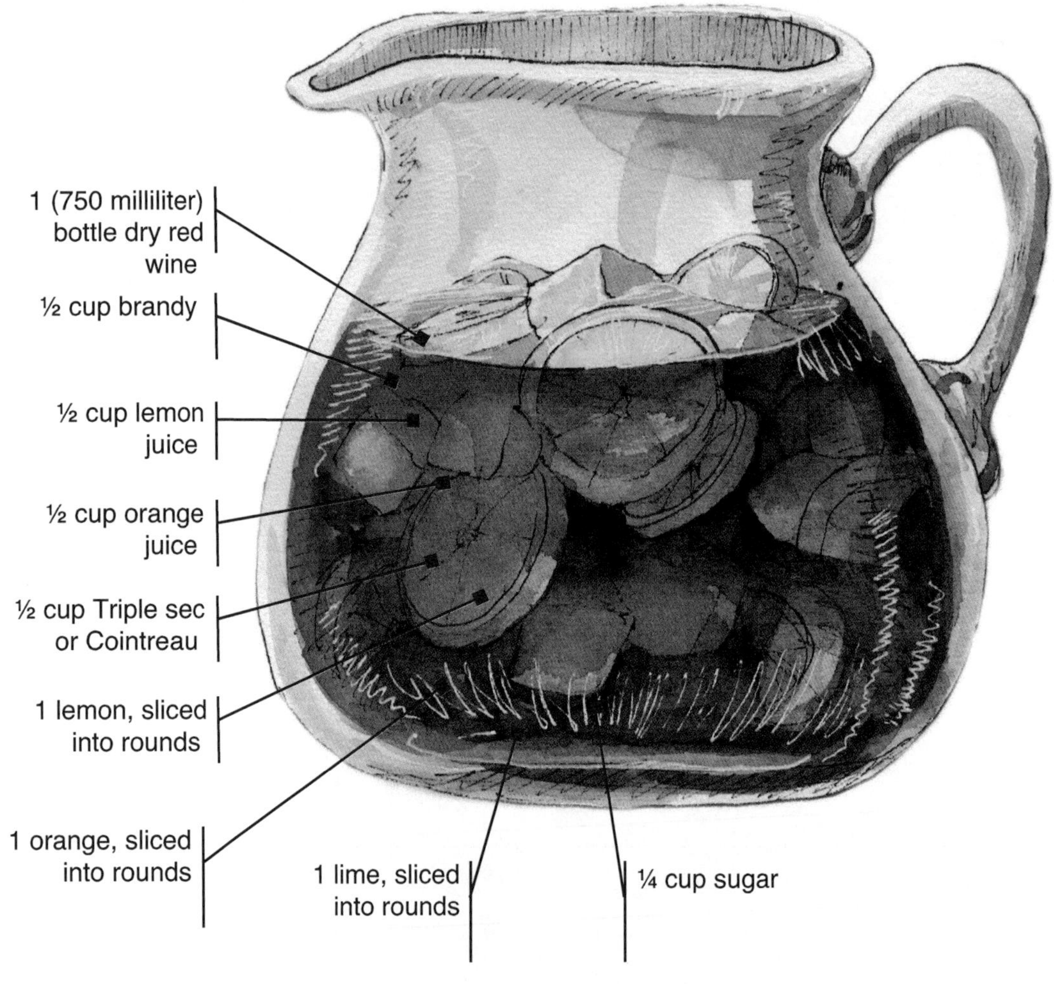
1 (750 milliliter) bottle dry red wine
½ cup brandy
½ cup lemon juice
½ cup orange juice
½ cup Triple sec or Cointreau
1 lemon, sliced into rounds
1 orange, sliced into rounds
1 lime, sliced into rounds
¼ cup sugar

Posh's Vineyard Sangria

Mix all ingredients in a large pitcher or bowl. Refrigerate overnight for best flavor.

TERRIFIC TIP

To make Ali's White Sangria, substitute a bottle of dry white wine and omit the brandy and lime.

Vineyard Menu

- Baguettes
- Cheese: cheddar, brie, gorgonzola, goat, manchego, provolone
- Charcuterie platter with cooked and dry-cured meats and sausage, garnished with olives and pickles
- Crackers and breadsticks
- Crudite/raw vegetable platter with grapes, strawberries, and apples
- Posh's Party Dips: Cheddar Blue Cheese Dip, Roasted Red Pepper Dip, Artichoke Blue Cheese Dip

TERRIFIC TIP

Don't forget to include Posh's signature cheese – Swiss! It's not a Posh Party without it.

Posh's Baguette Bar

Let your guests create a "baguette sandwich" with these ideas:

- Goat cheese or Boursin cheese as a base
- Toppings: roasted red peppers, sun dried tomatoes, pesto, honey, pecans, walnuts, pine nuts, olive oil, chili flakes, fleur de sel, blueberries, radishes, roasted corn, cherry tomatoes
- Selections from your cheese and charcuterie platters

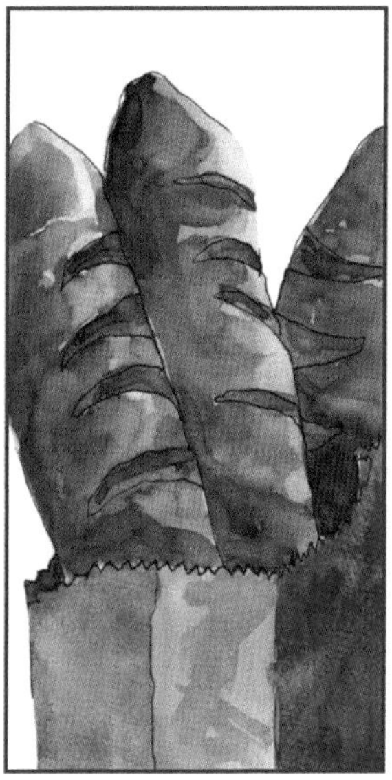

CHEEKY CHATTER

Posh ordered too many baguettes for a party, so he sent the extras home with guests as a special party favor.

TRICK
OR
TREAT

POSH TALK

I have a stellar collection of Halloween costumes – so many, that each year when I attend my favorite "Howlaween" party, I make multiple costume changes. Susan always goes with me to carry my suitcase of disguises, and sometimes we dress up as a team! One year, we were a big hit as Silver Shaded Persian kittens named Nick and Lexy after two of my dearest feline friends.

No matter what the season, when I visit Kennebunkport, I always take my lobster costume and my “crab dog hat” from Scalawags Pet Boutique. But I have the most fun when I summon my inner “spooky Posh” and pretend to be a vampire or pirate. No matter how I am dressed, my fans always recognize me as Posh, the Dog Star!

Dream without limits – plan a WICKED Howlaween party!

- Posh Proverb

7 Tricks for Treats

Set the Scene

Posh plans his Howlaween party for the patio and screened in porch so his guests can bring their canine friends, and all guests are expected to come dressed in costumes. His party theme is – Witches and Ghosts and Black Cats!

ZHIVAGO'S CREEPY CREATURES
GHOSTS
GOBLINS
VAMPIRES
WEREWOLVES
EAT
DRINK
BE SCARY
Calling All Witches, Ghosts, and Black Cats!
HOWLAWEEN PARTY
SATURDAY, OCT 31st
Celebration Begins at 5:00 p.m.
PRIZES!
BEST COSTUME
BEST OWNER/PET "COUPLE" COSTUME
RSVP IF YOU DARE:
Posh@properlyposhpets.com

TERRIFIC TIP

Take a picture of your pet in costume and tape it to the inside of a store-bought Halloween invitation.

Decorate with Witches and Ghosts and Black Cats – Oh My!

Find an old-fashioned "Magic 8-Ball" or decorate a glass bowl with glitter and fill it with fortunes that guests can select.

Put out bowls of Halloween candy – candy corn, red hots, and mini candy bars.

Decorate with lots of votive candles for atmosphere but make sure they are positioned out of the path of your canine party guests.

Stock a Disguise Bar with fun items like goofy glasses, self-stick moustaches, wax lips, and masks.

Spooktacular Playlist

Thriller – Michael Jackson

Monster Mash – Bobby Pickett and the Cryptkickers

Once Upon a Dream – Lana del Ray (remix)

Superstition – Stevie Wonder

Ghostbusters – Ray Parker, Jr.

Spooky – Dusty Springfield

Sweet Dreams (are made of this) – Marilyn Manson

Dance Magic Dance – David Bowie

Werewolves of London – Warren Zevon

Time Warp – Rocky Horror Picture Show

Scary Monsters and Super Creeps – David Bowie

Costume Contests

- Best Dog Costume
- Best Human Costume
- Best Dog/Owner "Couple"
- Most Creative Costume
- Scariest Costume
- Most Boo-tiful Costume
- Funniest Costume

Canine Contest Prizes

Bandanas: Buy several and let the contest winners pick their prize.

- Spooky
- Treat Junkie
- You Look Like I Could Use a Treat
- I Do Tricks for Treats
- Bad to the Bone
- Barking Bad

Human Contest Prizes

Fill a Trick or Treat basket with Halloween candy for contest winners to dive into for their prize.

BECKETT
BOO!

Gifts for Beckett and His Canine Guests

- "Wicked Cute" bandana
- Bag of "treats"
- Plush Halloween dog toys
- "Partner in Crime" collar

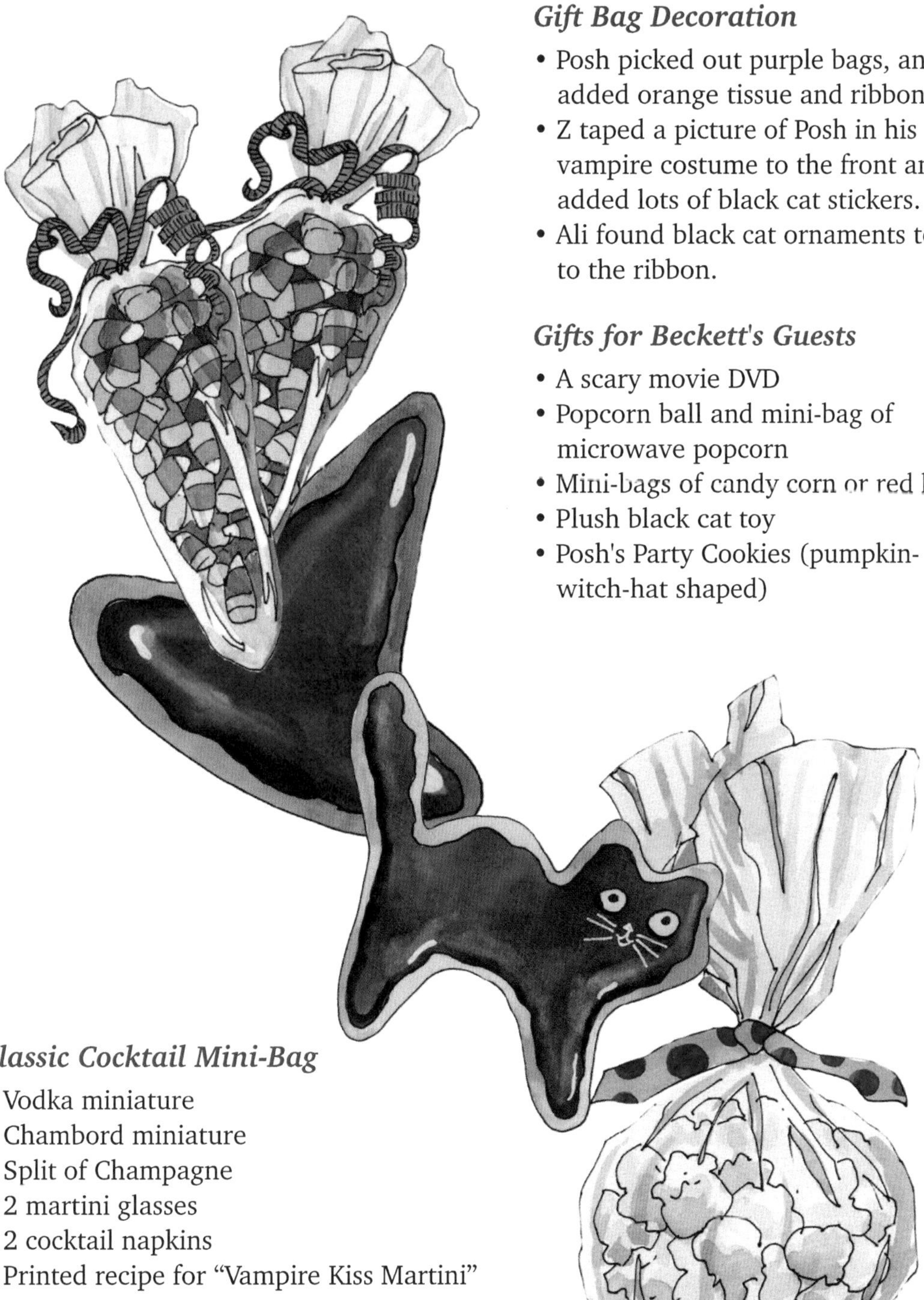

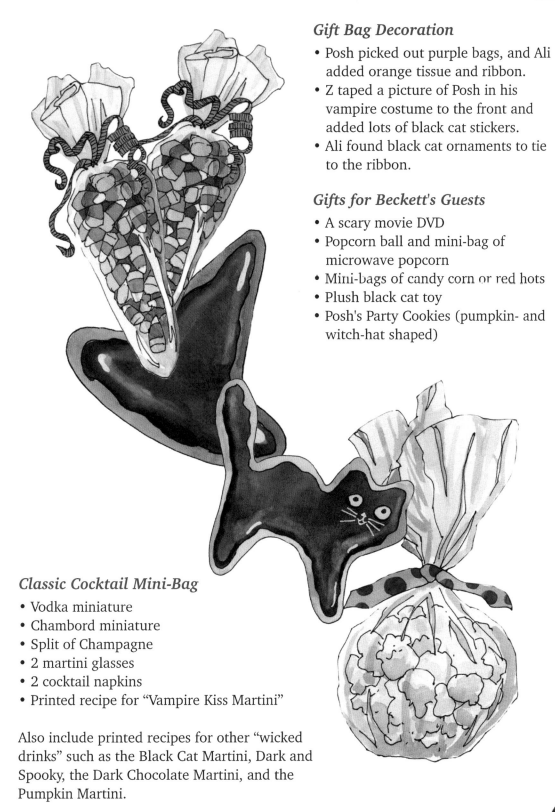

Gift Bag Decoration

- Posh picked out purple bags, and Ali added orange tissue and ribbon.
- Z taped a picture of Posh in his vampire costume to the front and added lots of black cat stickers.
- Ali found black cat ornaments to tie to the ribbon.

Gifts for Beckett's Guests

- A scary movie DVD
- Popcorn ball and mini-bag of microwave popcorn
- Mini-bags of candy corn or red hots
- Plush black cat toy
- Posh's Party Cookies (pumpkin- and witch-hat shaped)

Classic Cocktail Mini-Bag

- Vodka miniature
- Chambord miniature
- Split of Champagne
- 2 martini glasses
- 2 cocktail napkins
- Printed recipe for "Vampire Kiss Martini"

Also include printed recipes for other "wicked drinks" such as the Black Cat Martini, Dark and Spooky, the Dark Chocolate Martini, and the Pumpkin Martini.

Create the Classic Cocktail

Red sugar for rim of martini glass
1½ ounces vodka, chilled
1½ ounces Champagne
¾ ounce Chambord (black raspberry liqueur)

Vampire Kiss Martini

Rim the glass with red sugar. Pour vodka and half of the Chambord in a martini glass, and top with Champagne. Pour the rest of the Chambord over the back of a spoon to make it float.

CHEEKY CHATTER

Posh bought a Count Dracula costume for his first Howlaween party complete with cape and scary teeth. I have to stifle the giggles when he wears it now as he is far too cute to be a convincing vampire!

Spooktacular Menu

"Finger food" works well for this party:

- Mini mac and cheese
- Meatball sliders
- Mini cups of corn chowder
- "Bat" chicken wings
- Posh's Classic Cheese Fondue with vegetables and French bread
- "Spider" deviled eggs
- Chocolate cupcakes with black cat cupcake toppers
- Apple slices with caramel sauce
- Shortbread cookies dipped in dark chocolate with sea salt (witch hat-shaped)

TERRIFIC TIP

Posh thinks that lots of people LOVE burgers. He should know – he eats a burger every night for supper! So he asked me to design a "Sliders Bar" with burgers as an option.

Posh's Sliders Bar

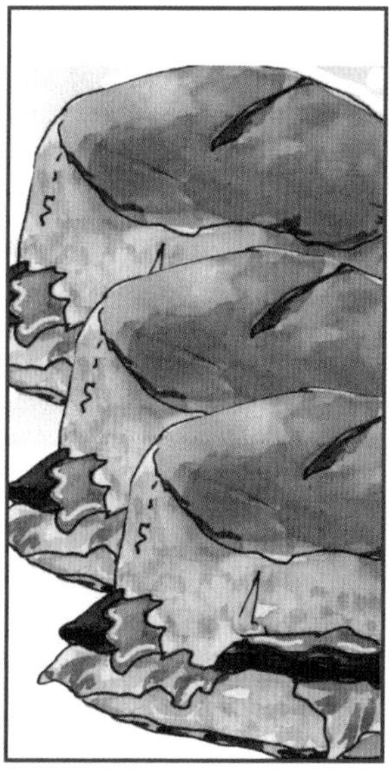

A fun way to provide a variety of "protein" options for your guests is to set up a "sliders" bar with mini-burgers and sandwiches using hamburger, meatballs, grilled chicken, grilled fish, and turkey or chicken burgers. Use store-bought slider buns and an assortment of toppings.

For toppings, include ketchup, mustard, tartar sauce, lettuce, tomato slices, onions, bell pepper rings, roasted red peppers, BBQ sauce, bacon, jalapeno slices, dill and sweet pickles, sweet pickle relish, mayonnaise, sautéed mushrooms, salsa, sriracha, avocado, and a variety of cheeses including Swiss, sharp cheddar, provolone, and blue.

O
T

POSH TALK

My name is Posh – but I wasn't named after a Spice Girl (although I love their music). Susan liked the word "posh" and thought it would be fun and easy to say. She was asked so many times if she named me after Posh Spice that she decided to register me with the AKC as "Beckham" (after a famous British footballer) – and my connection to football, both British and American was set.

Although I have never been to see my favorite team in person, you will find me sitting on the couch every Sunday afternoon during the fall – eating chips and Swiss cheese and barking "Touchdown!" Zhivago is the head cheerleader, and Ali always leads our team's fight song.

In a cat's eyes, all footballs belong to cats.

- Posh Proverb

8 Touchdown!

Set the Scene

Posh always throws at least one party every football season to show his loyalty to his favorite team – and as an excuse to treat his friends to the Rogers Family Chili and brownies.

Make your party educational!

- Print a guide of football terms to hand out to guests.
- Challenge your guests in a contest to explain football terms.
- Posh likes to include a couple of British football (aka soccer in the U.S.) terms such as "nutmeg" and "lifting the silverware".

ONSIDE KICK
Sack
ZONE DEFENSE
BLITZ
GAME PLAN
3:00 PM PRE-GAME
4:30 PM KICKOFF
ALL ACCESS PASS
TAILGATE and CELEBRATE!
DATE
NOV 27
TIME
3:00 PM
SECTION ROW SEAT
POSH'S PLACE
ARE YOU READY FOR SOME FOOTBALL?
PENALTY CALLED FOR FAILURE TO RSVP!

TERRIFIC TIP

This party can be adapted for other sports such as baseball, soccer, and basketball.

Use streamers and pompoms in the team colors and decorate with balloons with footballs or the team logo and colors.

Put a football banner and pennants on the front door of your home.

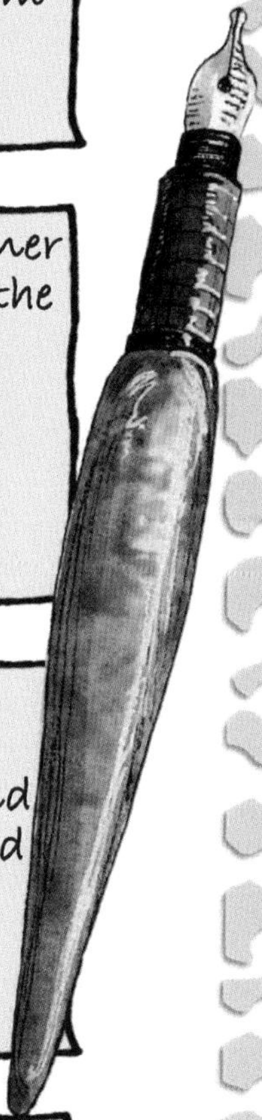

Buy or make a football field table cover or runner and use football-themed tableware (easily found online).

Look for creative ideas and materials to make scoreboards, football-shaped cakes and cookies, and goal posts.

Ask guests to wear your team's colors or clothing with their own favorite team's name, logo, or colors.

Kickoff the Party Playlist

We are the Champions/We Will Rock You – Queen

Who Let the Dogs Out – Baha Men

Don't Stop Believin – Journey

Celebration – Kool & the Gang

All My Rowdy Friends are Coming Over Tonight – Hank Williams, Jr.

Eye of the Tiger – Survivor

The Boys of Fall - Kenny Chesney

The Cup of Life – Ricky Martin (to celebrate Posh's connection to the game of "British football")

Don't forget to sing your team's Fight Song every time they score!

CHEEKY CHATTER

I always make sure one guest has the words to my team's fight song to lead the singing when the team scores!

Celebrate Your Pet

Pre-Game Activity

During the pre-game fun, you can play funny pet videos on the TV, such as "Puppy Bowl" or "Kitten Bowl" – you won't want to miss the penguin cheerleaders, the "tailgate" party, puppy spectators, and the kitten half-time show.

Show home movies or image slideshows of your pets.

Dress your pet in your team's logo with bandanas, T-shirts, and sweaters.

Gifts for Mason

- Dog toys – football, soccer ball
- Football rope toys
- Jersey for his favorite team
- Flying disk toys
- Team bandana
- Catnip football toys for the cats who stayed home
- Team mascot plush toy in team colors

TOUCHDOWN
INTERCEPTION
FUMBLE
TIME OUT
PUNT

GO
TEAM

Gift Bag Decoration

- Posh used a gold bag with red ribbon in his team's colors. Ali added red tissue.
- Decorate with football stickers and custom stickers of your pet.
- Z attached a football ornament to the ribbon.

Gifts for Mason's Guests

- Bags of peanuts and microwave popcorn
- A pair of pompoms
- Mini-football stress toy
- Dog sports movie DVD
- Posh's Party Cookies (football-shaped)

Classic Cocktail Mini-Bag

- 1 bottle of lager
- 1 bottle of hard cider
- 2 pint glasses
- 2 cocktail napkins
- Printed recipe for "The Red and Gold" (aka Snakebite)

Also include printed recipes for other beer cocktails such as the Black and Tan, the Black Velvet, and the Shandy.

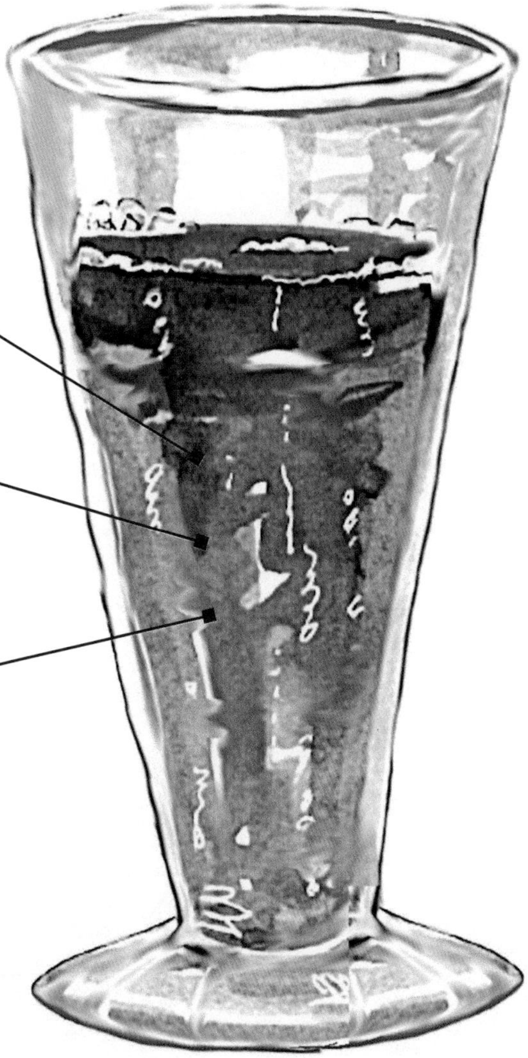
8 ounces lager, chilled
8 ounces hard cider, chilled
Dash of black currant liqueur (crème de cassis)

The Red and Gold (aka Snakebite)

Pour the cider and beer into a standard chilled pint glass.

To create a "Snakebite & Black," top with the black currant liqueur.

CHEEKY CHATTER

A pint of this beer cocktail goes down so easily that some pubs in London refuse to make it!

Game Day Menu

- Rogers Family Chili with "fixins": beans, onions, cheddar cheese, sour cream, red pepper flakes, tortilla chips
- Vegetarian chili
- Cornbread
- Chips and dip (onion, guacamole, and salsa)
- Crudite/raw vegetable platter
- Brownies
- Beer, cider, mulled wine

TERRIFIC TIP

Sprinkle colored glitter sugar in your team's colors on the tops of your brownies.

Posh's Popcorn Bar

This is a fun and easy idea for a party that allows guests to personalize their own bag of popcorn.

Pre-order bags of two or three basic popcorn flavors from a local popcorn store or pop your own before the party.

Seasonings: kettle corn, nacho cheddar, ranch, caramel, chili lime, and a butter spritzer.

POSH TALK

Over the past 10 years, my parties have become more and more fabulous, but there have been a handful of party recipes that have become my "signature" party foods. My friends encouraged me to share some of these recipes – and, in fact, my friend Diane said that she would buy my book just to get my Posh Party Cookie recipe. How could I refuse?

Some of my "signature party foods" are from recipes handed down to Susan from her mom Carol who loved to cook – and eat – and drink – and party! We decided to share some of those recipes. We hope that you will enjoy the Rogers Chicken Casserole and Rogers Family Chili with Fixins.

When you are using these recipes, don't forget to sprinkle a little "Posh Magic" – use your own creativity to turn my recipes into your signature dishes by adding your own special ideas to the mix.

In the cookies of life, dogs are the chocolate chips and cats are the nuts.

- Posh Proverb

9 Posh's Party Recipes

CHEF
CUDDY

Posh's Party Cookies

Ingredients – Sugar Cookies

½ cup butter
1 cup sugar
2 medium eggs
½ teaspoon salt
2 teaspoons baking powder
2 cups flour
½ teaspoon vanilla

Directions

- Cream butter and sugar. Blend in eggs.
- Add salt, baking powder, and flour. Add vanilla.
- Refrigerate. Roll to a quarter-inch thickness.
- Using cookie cutters, cut into desired shapes for your party theme.
- Bake at 400° for 8-10 minutes.
- Frost with Vanilla Butter Frosting.

Ingredients – Vanilla Butter Frosting

1½ cups (3 sticks) unsalted butter (melt 2½ sticks and soften ½ stick)
4½ - 5½ cups confectioners sugar
½ cup milk
3 teaspoons vanilla

Directions

- Combine the melted and softened butter in a large mixing bowl.
- Add 4 cups of sugar, then add the milk and vanilla.
- On medium speed, beat until smooth and creamy for 4-5 minutes.
- Slowly add the remaining sugar, a half cup at a time, beating well after each addition until the icing is thick and easily spreadable. You may not need to add all of the sugar to achieve the proper consistency.
- Add a few drops of food coloring in order to match the cookie frosting to the color scheme of your party.
- Frost your cooled cookies immediately and decorate.

Posh's Party Cake

Ingredients

1 box white angel food cake mix
1¼ cups cold water
3 cups of whipping cream (1½ pints)
4 tablespoons of sugar
Red food coloring

Directions

- Move oven rack to lowest position (remove other racks). Heat oven to 350°F. In an extra-large glass or metal bowl, beat cake mix and cold water with electric mixer on low speed 30 seconds. Beat on medium speed 1 minute. Pour into ungreased 10" angel food heart-shaped (tube) cake pan. (Do not use fluted tube cake pan or 9" angel food pan or batter will overflow.)
- Bake 37 to 47 minutes or until top is dark golden brown and cracks feel very dry and are not sticky. Do not under-bake. Immediately turn the pan upside down over a glass bottle or invert on feet attached to the pan. Cool the cake completely.
- In medium bowl, beat whipping cream on high speed until stiff peaks form. Fold sugar into whipping cream. Fold in red food coloring to tint the whipped cream pink.
- On serving plate, place cake with browned side down. Frost top and sides of cake with whipped cream frosting. Refrigerate until served.

Option

Serve with fresh strawberries.

Variations

This is a good cake to use for any party since your dog can eat a tiny piece to join in the fun and your cat will love a tiny bit of whipped cream. Tint the whipped cream frosting a color to match your party color scheme and use a different shaped pan to fit your theme.

Posh's Magical Fudge

Ingredients

¾ cup butter
3 cups sugar
5 ounces evaporated milk
12 ounce package semi-sweet chocolate chips
7 ounce jar marshmallow cream
1 teaspoon vanilla

Directions

- Grease a 9" x 13" pan.
- Combine butter, sugar, and milk in a large, heavy saucepan over medium heat. Bring to a boil, and stir constantly to dissolve sugar. Boil for 5 minutes.
- Remove from heat, and stir in chocolate chips until melted and thoroughly combined.
- With a wooden spoon, beat in marshmallow cream and vanilla.
- Spoon fudge into prepared pan and let cool before cutting into squares.

Variations

- Add nuts such as pecans, walnuts, pistachios, or macadamia nuts, and consider lightly toasting them.
- Add plain or lightly toasted coconut or dried cherries.
- Use mint chocolate chips for Mint Chocolate Fudge.
- For Rocky Road Fudge, add tiny marshmallows and walnuts after the chocolate and marshmallow cream are thoroughly blended.
- Pour the fudge into individual pans in different shapes, such as hearts, to match your party theme.
- Decorate the top of your fudge with candy pieces, nuts, orange zest, sea salt (on dark chocolate fudge), or candy canes (with peppermint extract in the mix).

Posh's Birthday Cake

Ingredients - Golden Butter Cake

1 butter golden box cake mix
½ cup of water
3 large eggs
7 tablespoons softened butter

Directions

- Preheat oven to 350° for metal or glass pans, 325° for dark or coated pans. Use a bone-shaped sheet cake pan. Grease sides and bottom of each pan with shortening or oil spray. Flour lightly.
- Blend cake mix, water, softened butter, and eggs in large bowl at low speed until moistened (about 30 seconds). Beat at medium speed for 4 minutes.
- Pour batter in pan and bake immediately for 26-31 minutes. Cake is done when toothpick inserted in center comes out clean.
- Cool in pan on wire rack for 15 minutes. Cool completely before frosting.

Ingredients - Caramel Frosting

2 cups (4 sticks) unsalted butter, softened
3-4 cups of sifted confectioners sugar
1½ cups firmly packed dark brown sugar
½ cup milk
2 tablespoons dark corn syrup
2 teaspoons vanilla

Directions

- Using the medium speed of an electric mixer, cream the butter in a large bowl until smooth.
- Add the confectioners and brown sugar and beat on low speed for 2 minutes.
- Add the milk, corn syrup, and vanilla, and beat until smooth and creamy for 3-5 minutes.
- Frost the cooled cake immediately.
- Decorate with bone-shaped candles.

Rogers Chicken Casserole

Ingredients

5-6 chicken breasts (baked or boiled but don't overcook)
1 carton (16 ounces) sour cream
1 can of cream of chicken soup
1½ cups breadcrumbs
½ cup (1 stick) butter
Poppy seeds

Directions

- Bake or boil the chicken breasts until tender but not dry. Tear the chicken meat into bite-sized pieces.
- Combine the sour cream and cream of chicken soup. Mix well and add to the chicken.
- Put the mixture into a casserole dish.
- Melt the butter and add the breadcrumbs. Spread the mixture on the top of the chicken in the casserole.
- Sprinkle poppy seeds generously over the top of the casserole.
- Bake at 350° for 25-30 minutes until brown and bubbly.

Variations

- Use dark and white meat of the chicken.
- Add mushrooms, broccoli, spinach, or carrots.
- Serve with noodles or biscuits and fresh peas.

Posh's Clam Chowder

Posh has a favorite “take-out” restaurant in Kennebunkport, Maine, called Alisson’s. They make an excellent clam chowder mix that can be purchased from the store or online. It includes the clams and the chowder base, and all you do is add cream and butter and cook. That way you have more time for walks with your dog!

But if you are feeling ambitious, here is Posh’s recipe for a traditional clam chowder with ideas for variations on the basic recipe.

Ingredients

3 (6½ ounce) cans minced clams
1 cup minced onion
1 cup celery
2 cups cubed potatoes
1 cup diced carrots
¾ cup butter
¾ cup all-purpose flour
1 quart half-and-half cream
2 tablespoons red wine vinegar
1½ teaspoons salt
Ground black pepper to taste

Directions

- Drain juice from the clams into a large frypan over the onions, celery, potatoes, and carrots. Add water to cover, and cook over medium heat until tender.
- In a large, heavy saucepan, melt the butter over medium heat. Whisk in flour until smooth. Whisk in cream and stir constantly until thick and smooth.
- Stir in vegetables and clam juice. Heat through, but do not boil.
- Stir in clams just before serving (so they don’t get tough). When the clams are heated through, stir in the vinegar, and season with salt and pepper.
- Serve with oyster crackers!

Additions: Add bacon, green onions, hot pepper sauce, asparagus, sliced tomatoes, and carrots
Other seasonings: Old Bay, parsley, and paprika

Variations

- Seafood or fish chowder using shrimp, scallops, crabmeat, monkfish, or cod
- Manhattan chowder, which has a red broth and is tomato-based
- Shrimp and corn chowder

Serve all of these dips with a selection of crackers, French bread, pita chips, or raw vegetables.

Cheddar Blue Cheese Dip

Combine equal parts of cheddar cheese, blue cheese, and cream cheese.

Artichoke Blue Cheese Dip

Combine ½ cup blue cheese dressing, 15 ounces of artichoke hearts (drained and chopped), 8 ounces of sour cream, and 2 green onions (chopped). Chill for 1 hour.

Roasted Red Pepper Dip

Combine 1 cup (12 ounces) of canned roasted red peppers (drained), 1 cup of sour cream, 1 tablespoon of chopped fresh basil, 2 garlic cloves (peeled and chopped), ½ teaspoon of salt, and ¼ teaspoon of black pepper in a food processor or blender. Refrigerate until served.

Warm Crab Dip

In a 3-quart saucepan, heat ½ cup (1 stick) of butter, 8 ounces of cream cheese, ¼ cup sour cream, and ¼ teaspoon of cayenne (ground red) pepper over medium heat for 6 minutes, stirring constantly until the mixture is smooth and warm. Fold in 12-16 ounces of fresh crabmeat (with shells removed), 2 green onions or scallions (thinly sliced), 2 tablespoons of parsley, and 2 teaspoons of lemon juice and heat another minute, then serve.

Posh's Baked Feta

Posh has a favorite wine bar in Kennebunkport, Maine, where he loves to sit by the fire pits on the patio in the fall – eating his favorite Swiss cheese while Susan enjoys their Baked Feta. If you want to serve this at your party, here is Posh's recipe, but you need to eat it as soon as you bake it, so this is best suited for a party at home.

1¾-inch-thick block of feta
Pinch of crushed red pepper and a pinch of dried oregano
2 tablespoons extra-virgin olive oil
Crusty bread or toasted pita chips for serving
2-3 lemon wedges

Heat the oven to 350°. Put the feta in a small baking dish and sprinkle the red pepper flakes and oregano over the cheese. Drizzle with 1 tablespoon of the olive oil and bake until softened, about 10 minutes. Drizzle with more olive oil and serve with the bread and toasted pita chips with lemon wedges to squeeze on the cheese.

Posh's Classic Cheese Fondue

Ingredients

1 garlic clove, halved
¾ cup dry white wine
1 tablespoon lemon juice
10 ounces Emmental cheese, grated
10 ounces Gruyere cheese, grated
1 tablespoon cornstarch
1 teaspoon mustard powder
2 tablespoons Kirsch
Pepper to taste

Directions

- Rub the inside of the fondue pot with the garlic, then discard.
- Pour the wine and lemon juice into the fondue pot and bring to a boil on a stove burner, then reduce the heat so that the liquid is at a simmer. Gradually add the Emmental cheese and Gruyere cheese, stirring constantly until all the cheese is combined.
- Blend the cornstarch, mustard powder, and kirsch and add to the fondue. Cook at low temperature for 2-3 minutes, then season to taste with pepper.
- Transfer the fondue pot to its tabletop burner and serve with cubes of crusty French bread and a variety of other options listed above.

Dippers

- Cubes of crusty French bread or cubes of other types of bread such as brown bread
- Vegetables such as cherry tomatoes, snowpeas, and red peppers or steamed broccoli, zucchini, baby carrots, cauliflower, and asparagus
- Chunks of ham and sausage
- Jumbo shrimp

Variations

Cheese variations: Cheddar, edam, gouda, fontina, vacherin, pecorino, and provolone
Alcohol variations: Cider, beer, brandy, or Champagne
Spice variations: Sun-dried tomatoes, cayenne, cumin, or caraway

Rogers Family Chili

Ingredients

1½ pounds ground beef
1 large onion chopped
1 green pepper chopped
3 tablespoon chili powder
1 teaspoon sugar
1 large or 2 medium cans tomatoes including juice (crush whole tomatoes with fork)
1 small can tomato paste
Salt and pepper to taste

Directions

- Brown meat and onion. Skim off fat.
- Add rest of ingredients.
- Bring to a boil, then reduce heat and cook at least an hour.
- Add water if needed.

Variations

- "Fixins" for chili can be offered on your food table including: red kidney beans or black beans, chopped onions, corn, cheddar cheese, sour cream, red pepper flakes, sliced avocado, and tortilla chips.
- Consider offering a chicken chili with white beans or a vegetarian chili with corn and kidney, garbanzo, or black beans.

POSH TALK

My little sister Ali asked if she could be the "guest co-editor" for this Posh Talk. Since she is the Posh Princess of all things Glitter and Glam, I said "Go for it, Ali!" When it comes to the invitations, we both think that plastering our pictures all over the invite is the way to go – what better way to showcase the STAR of your party and give your guests a hint of the celebration and fun to come on the big day.

For decorations and tableware, Ali and I agree that it is practical to invest in some basic decorations, such as mini-string lights and neutral colored plates, which you can use for multiple parties, and then you can focus on a manageable list of decorations that are specific to the theme of your party – and go WILD with imagination!

In Ali's world, you can never spend too much time or money on selecting pet couture and costumes – or deciding on the special Posh Presents to shower on your Pet of Honor. And then we come to Ali's favorite category – Bags and Ribbon – which is all a Posh Princess of Presents needs to create magical, glamorous gift bags for her special guests.

Ali says I am the master of all things food so I have created that list of resources. Ali and I decided to put Z in charge of "Ideas" – he is still developing that list and will continue to add information to our website.

Ali, Z, and I all love getting ready for the party – the anticipation of the good times we will have and the wonderful friends we will see is a very big part of the fun of entertaining for us. When all is said and done after the party, we love to "Paws and Remember" – and then start to "Paws and Plan" for the next Posh Party!

If you dream the magic, you can create the magic.

- Posh Proverb

10 Posh's Party Resources

Invitations/Custom Items

Cafe Press
www.cafepress.com

Evermine
www.evermine.com

Evite
www.evite.com

For Your Party
www.foryourparty.com

Hallmark
www.hallmark.com

Mark and Graham
www.markandgraham.com

Merrimade
www.merrimade.com

Minted
www.minted.com

Mixbook
www.mixbook.com

Oriental Trading Company
www.orientaltrading.com

Paper Source
www.papersource.com

Paper Style
www.paperstyle.com

Paperless Post
www.paperless.com

Party City
www.partycity.com

Shutterfly
www.shutterfly.com

Staples
www.staples.com

Tiny Prints
www.tinyprints.com

Vistaprint
www.vistaprint.com

Decorations/Tableware

Bags & Bows
www.bagsandbowsonline.com

Birthday Express
www.birthdayexpress.com

Celebrate Express
www.celebrateexpress.com

Crate and Barrel
www.crateandbarrel.com

Fancy Flours
www.fancyflours.com

Michaels
www.michaels.com

Oriental Trading
www.orientialtrading.com

Paper Mart
www.papermart.com

Paper Source
www.papersource.com

Party City
www.partycity.com

Pottery Barn
www.potterybarn.com

Royer
Swizzle sticks
shop.royercorp.com

Shindigz
www.shindigz.com

Smartpack
Swizzle sticks
www.smartpackusa.com

Sur La Table
www.surlatable.com

Target
www.target.com

Wayfair
www.wayfair.com

Zazzle
www.zazzle.com

Pet Toys, Clothes & Products

Barkshop
www.barkshop.com

Chewy
www.chewy.com

Dog.com
www.dog.com

Fanatics
Sports
www.fanatics.com

Fetch Dog
In the Company of Dogs
www.fetchdog.com

I See Spot
www.iseespot.com

Mary Lake Thompson
www.marylakethompson.com

Petco
www.petco.com

Petsmart
www.petsmart.com

Scalawags
Pet Store
www.scalawagsonline.com

The Dog Perk
Bandanas
www.thedogperk.com
www.fundogbandanas.com

Two Salty Dogs
Woofie Pies
www.twosaltydogs.com

Wylie Wagg
Pet Store
www.wyliewagg.com

Zazzle
www.zazzle.com

Gift Wrap & Ribbon

Bags & Bows
www.bagsandbowsonline.com

Birthday Express
www.birthdayexpress.com

Container Store
www.containerstore.com

Hallmark
www.hallmark.com

Michaels
www.michaels.com

Oriental Trading
www.orientaltrading.com

Paper Mart
www.papermart.com

Paper Source
www.papersource.com

Target
www.target.com

Zazzle
www.zazzle.com

Uline
www.uline.com

Food

Alisson's
Clam chowder mix
www.alissons.com

Cake Art
www.cakeart.com

Fancy Flours
www.fancyflours.com

King Arthur Flour
www.kingarthurflour.com

Michaels
www.michaels.com

Stonewall Kitchen
www.stonewallkitchen.com

Sur La Table
www.surlatable.com

The Bakers Kitchen
www.thebakerskitchen.com

Williams Sonoma
www.williamssonoma.com

Wilton
www.wilton.com

Miscellaneous

Amazon
Invitations, decorations, pet products
www.amazon.com

Home Depot
Mini-string lights
www.homedepot.com

Lowes
Mini-string lights
www.lowes.com

MyPix2.com
Posters, photobooks, canvas prints
www.mypix2.com

Snapfish
Photo cards, custom photobooks
www.snapfish.com

Sources for Ideas

Google
www.google.com

Pinterest
www.pinterest.com

Properly Posh Pets
www.properlyposhpets.com
Zhivago is working hard on more "idea sources" and will add them on our website as he identifies them.

Posh's Party Checklist

Posh and I have developed this checklist over the years using our experiences from many parties. We keep several copies of the list on hand, so that we can use one copy as a checklist for each party that we plan. It's especially useful on the day of the party to keep the food preparation organized and make sure that Posh is ready at the front door when the guests start arriving! This list is customized to our house, but you can use our categories to create your own standard list for the parties you give.

Before the Party

Write out your menu
Write out your grocery list

House Preparations

Vacuum and dust
Check guest bathroom
Put a clean throw rug at front door
Turn on outside lights in the front and back of house
Check garden for dead plants
Scoop litter boxes!
Light candles
Pick up towels used on furniture for protection against pet hair
Sweep porches
Arrange flowers
Check fireplaces

Posh Preparations

Bath
Pick out collar, leash, bandana and other clothes/costumes

Food and Alcohol Preparations

Put wine and other drinks in the refrigerator
Collect glasses for your wine, beer, and other beverages
Find wine opener, shot glass, and beer opener
Get supplies out for coffee and tea (including sugar and cream)
Find salt and pepper shakers
Collect silverware and plates
Arrange napkins and tablecloths

Miscellaneous

Prepare music, including CD selection
Organize and set up your entertainment and activities

Guest Dog Credits

***Beckett** (Hound Group Representative)*

Beckett is a Hound mix who lives in Upperville, Virginia with Diane Arnold. He is an athletic, graceful dog who loves to roam the Virginia countryside – and "howl" at the moon when he attends the "Tricks for Treats" party.

***Boomer** (Working Group Representative)*

Boomer is a Boxer who lives in Woodbridge, Virginia with Monica and Bruce Herdt. He is a highly intelligent, boisterous dog who loves his weekly visits to "doggy daycare." He provided a variety of ideas for the "Paws to Celebrate" chapter.

***Cuddy** (Goldendoodle Group Representative)*

Cuddy is a Golden Retriever-Poodle mix who lives in Wells, Maine with Cathy and Tom Norton. He is friendly and playful, which are great qualities for a dog with a full-time job as Kennebunkport Marina mascot. He volunteered to "captain" the "Posh Party Recipes" chapter.

JACK

***Jack** (Terrier Group Representative)*

Jack is a Wheaten Terrier who lives in Kennebunkport, Maine with Mary Beth Kvaka and Bill Fisher. He is affectionate, gentle, and loving with a passion for car rides and day tripping. He agreed to help with the "Vines, Wines, Fun Times!" party but he would rather have ice cream than wine!

***Mason** (Hound Group Representative)*

Mason is a Long-Haired Miniature Dachshund who lives in Johns Creek, Georgia with Dawn, Darrell and Landon Rogers. He is a clever and entertaining dog who never misses an Auburn University football game, so he was the perfect assistant for the "Touchdown" party – War Eagle!

***Remy** (Terrier Group Representative)*

Remy is an American Pit Bull Terrier who lives with Laura and Bob Honohan in Warrenton, Virginia. Remy is an affectionate and playful dog who recently discovered that boating is great fun, so she is the perfect volunteer for the "Life's a Beach!" party.

***Rose** (Terrier Group Representative)*

Rose was a Wheaten Terrier who shared a home with Jack, Mary Beth and Bill in Kennebunkport, Maine. She was a free-spirited, loving dog who had a passion for the beach and had the chance to fulfill that passion for many years with daily walks along the ocean.

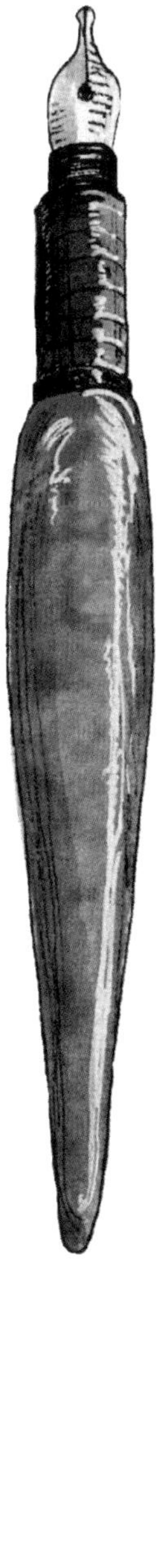

Party Planning Notes

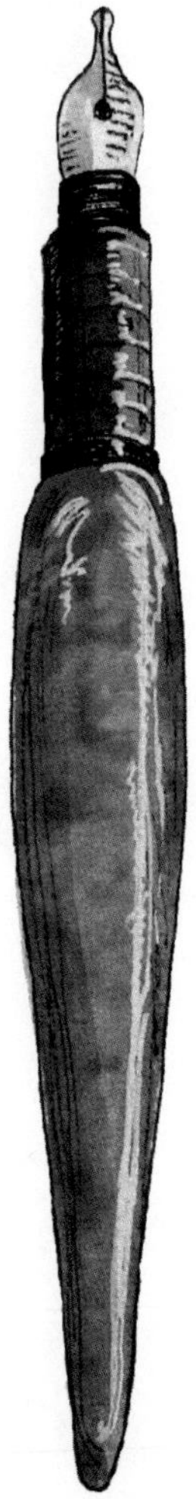

65178896R00053

Made in the USA
Charleston, SC
12 December 2016